Ralph Gagne
6047 Fauntleroy
WEST 2-7055

SUNRISE AT CAMPOBELLO

Sunrise at Campobello

A PLAY IN THREE ACTS

BY

Dore Schary

RANDOM HOUSE
NEW YORK

FOURTH PRINTING

Photographs by courtesy of Friedman-Abeles

Library of Congress Catalog Card Number: 58–7672

Manufactured in the United States of America

For My Best Friend

MIRIAM

FOREWORD

Last January I made up my mind to write *Sunrise at Campobello.* I had read everything that had been written about Franklin D. Roosevelt since his death and I had on numerous occasions felt that there was a moving and dramatic tale to be told concerning the years of his illness, but I had not yet applied either my energy or my time to truly study the material as a source for a play. Now I had the time and, hopefully, the energy.

I went to work and almost immediately determined that the final image in the play was to be the figure of FDR standing at the podium in Madison Square Garden on the afternoon of June 26, 1924, when he nominated Alfred E. Smith as the Presidential candidate for the Democratic Party. It was that dramatic appearance which changed the course of FDR's life, and consequently, the lives of so many Americans. On that day in his speech he delivered the famous "Happy Warrior" phrase (a quote from a poem by William Wordsworth and suggested by Joseph Proskauer), and in one stroke disabused his party of the notion that he was incapable of public service and became, in the opinion of political columnists of that era, the most attractive political personality of his time.

Only thirty-four months before his dynamic renascence, he had been stricken with infantile paralysis and suffered permanent crippling of his legs. The story of those thirty-four months would, I felt, tell a story of challenge and response, of defeat and despair, turned into victory and confidence.

The characters were almost fiction-like in their dramaturgical potential. FDR, rising from the crucible of pain to become, eventually, a four-time President of the United States; his wife Eleanor, an awkward and shy young woman, who in these months was forged by circumstances which ultimately made her the First Lady of the world; Louis McHenry Howe, a homely man, an eccentric asthmatic who maintained a vigil of devotion and lived to see his prophecy (made in 1912, that FDR would become President) come true. There was a house full of children. Also, there was the matriarchal Sara Delano Roosevelt, who had contempt for politics and who, deeply anxious for her son during his illness, strongly urged him to retire to Hyde Park and the life of a country squire. Finally, there was the rich and saucy character of Alfred E. Smith and the part he played in the climax of these three years.

The incidents were considerable. There was a magnificent bibliography, the Hyde Park Library bursting with details and records, and, finally, the personal recollections of the Roosevelt family.

I had the final scene first. The initial scene in the play came next to mind. That would be the day he took ill at Campobello, August 10, 1921. The title (in Thornton Wilder's figure of speech) came down my arm to the pencil—*Sunrise at Campobello*. All I needed was three acts of playwrighting.

I made some obvious decisions early in the game. Al Smith would never say "raddio" and he wouldn't wear a brown derby. FDR would not say "My friends." But I still had three acts to write.

The material was sifted and selected. Relationships were probed and studied. Significant quotes were placed in chronological sequence. I charted the details: the day and manner in which he was carried from Campobello; the first day he wore his leg braces and when he started on his crutches; the clothes he wore and his favorite poems and readings; the fears he had and his faith in God; his conflicts with his mother; his business ventures and his wrong guesses (such as his conviction that Herbert Hoover would be the Democratic candidate in 1924); the way he crawled; and the exact dimensions of the kitchen chairs he reconstructed into wheel chairs.

I culled the letters that might be used and the fragments of remembered dialogue that might cue me to the way he talked in private conversation during that period. I came to know his choice colors and those of Mrs. Roosevelt. I learned about Louis Howe's favorite cigarettes. (Sweet Caporals); FDR's indignation because of the bigotry so nakedly exposed against Al Smith; FDR's explanations of his illness to his children so that they would have no unspoken fears of it; Eleanor's first plunge into public speaking at the blunt prodding of Louis Howe; and I became familiar with scads of names, dates and events.

But I was still three acts away from a play.

One day in May, I was ready for that frightening yet tremendously exciting moment when you sit down and write tentatively and hopefully—Act One, Scene 1.

The characters and happenings began to slip into place. The dialogue moved me into the era of some thirty-seven years ago, and I was on the way.

What has been written is true. Dramatic needs forced me to compress and to edit some of the events, but if the play has force and emotion it is because the real people lived these days with force and emotion.

In March, 1957, I wrote Mrs. Roosevelt asking for permission to do this play. My letter read in part, "What I propose to tell is the story of a man and the people around him who, after an ordeal, emerged strong and triumphant. I hope to write a tribute that will do justice to a phase of his life. I pledge my devotion and whatever skill I may have to do the task."

I hope, with all my heart, that the task is well done.

January 14, 1958 DORE SCHARY

I take this opportunity to acknowledge the invaluable aid received from personal recollections and comments by Mrs. Eleanor Roosevelt, Mrs. James Halsted, Congressman James Roosevelt and Mr. Franklin D. Roosevelt, Jr.

I also extend deep appreciation to the authors of the vast bibliography concerning the life, times and works of Franklin D. Roosevelt.

Finally, my sincere thanks to Dr. Herman Kahn, director of the Hyde Park Memorial Library, and to his assistant, Raymond Corry, and to the entire staff of the Library for their constant guidance and aid.

SUNRISE AT CAMPOBELLO *was first presented by The Theatre Guild and Dore Schary at the Cort Theatre, New York City, on January 30, 1958, with the following cast:*

(IN ORDER OF APPEARANCE)

ANNA ROOSEVELT	Roni Dengel
ELEANOR ROOSEVELT	Mary Fickett
FRANKLIN D. ROOSEVELT, JR.	Kenneth Kakos
JAMES ROOSEVELT	James Bonnet
ELLIOTT ROOSEVELT	Perry Skaar
EDWARD	James Earl Jones
FRANKLIN DELANO ROOSEVELT	Ralph Bellamy
JOHN ROOSEVELT	Jeffrey Rowland
MARIE	Ethel Everett
LOUIS MCHENRY HOWE	Henry Jones
MRS. SARA DELANO ROOSEVELT	Anne Seymour
MISS MARGUERITE (MISSY) LEHAND	Mary Welch
DOCTOR BENNET	James Reese
FRANKLIN CALDER	William Fort
STRETCHER BEARERS	Edwin Phillips, Vincent Dowling, Floyd Curtis
MR. BRIMMER	Clifford Carpenter
MR. LASSITER	Richard Robbins
GOVERNOR ALFRED E. SMITH	Alan Bunce
DALY	Jerry Crews
POLICEMAN	Floyd Curtis
SENATOR WALSH	Vincent Dowling
A SPEAKER	Edwin Phillips

Directed by Vincent J. Donehue

Production designed and lighted by Ralph Alswang

Costumes by Virginia Volland

Act One

Scene 1. The living room of the Franklin D. Roosevelt home at Campobello, New Brunswick, Canada, August 10, 1921.

Scene 2. The same, September 1, 1921.

Scene 3. The same, September 13, 1921.

Act Two

Scene 1. The living room of the Franklin D. Roosevelt home in New York, May, 1922.

Scene 2. The same, January, 1923.

Act Three

Scene 1. The same, May, 1924.

Scene 2. Madison Square Garden (an anteroom), June 26, 1924.

Scene 3. The platform, moments later.

ACT ONE

ACT ONE

SCENE ONE

Scene: It is August 10, 1921. We are in the large living room of the FRANKLIN DELANO ROOSEVELT *summer home at Campobello, New Brunswick, Canada. It is a homey, sprawling summer lodge. Picture windows reveal the firs and pines of the forest and allow us to view part of the bay. The sky is pink with the coming dusk. A porch runs along outside the house and we can see some of it. The entire atmosphere is woodsy and comfortable, not elegant or fancy, but rather, a house that has seen hard wear by an energetic and healthy family. There are no electric lights. At night the house is illuminated by kerosene lamps, many of which are placed about the room.*

At rise: The stage is empty. Then ANNA ROOSEVELT, *wearing a bathing suit and carrying a picnic basket, can be glimpsed coming across the porch.*

ANNA (*As she comes into the house*) Mother! (*Then louder*) Mother!

(MRS. ELEANOR ROOSEVELT *appears on the steps leading down into the room. She is a tall, stately and willowy young woman of thirty-six. She is dressed in a white flannel skirt and blue sweater and wears white sneakers. She looks warm and a bit disheveled*)

ELEANOR Yes, Anna.

ANNA Mother, you missed all the fun. After sailing, we went swimming in the lagoon and then we trotted across the spit and dove into the bay.

ELEANOR It sounds very strenuous. I am delighted that I never learned how to swim. (*She motions* ANNA *upstairs.* ANNA *smiles and starts up the steps*) If you're through with the picnic I'd better take the basket.

(ANNA *smiles, hands* ELEANOR *the basket and continues up the steps.* FRANKLIN JR., *wearing a bathing suit, storms in and throws his towel and his sweater down near the clothes rack*)

FRANKLIN JR. (*Wearily*) Hello, Mother.

ELEANOR Hello, young Franklin. (*He crosses to the couch and collapses*) Franklin, I know that you're on the verge of exhaustion, but you are to get up from that couch and put your towel and sweater where they belong.

FRANKLIN JR. (*Questioningly*) Now?

ELEANOR Now.

(FRANKLIN JR. *groans his way from the couch, picks up the sweater and towel, puts them on the rack, and then staggers back in the direction of the couch.* ELEANOR *looks at him and crosses stage right to the study off the living room.* JIMMY *and* ELLIOTT *now enter from the porch. Both of them are also wearing bathing suits. They too toss their towels and sweaters more or less in the direction of the clothes rack*)

JIMMY (*To* ELLIOTT) You paddle your way along like a polliwog. Your hands have to hit the water clean—(*He illustrates*) That's the only way to get pull into your stroke—like this when you come back.

ELLIOTT You aren't exactly champion of the world, you know.

JIMMY I'm only telling you what Pa told me. He told it to all of us, but you don't listen. Elliott, you never listen.

(*By now* ELLIOTT *has become aware of* FRANKLIN JR., *stretched out on the couch, and he silently indicates to* JIMMY *that they do something about this.* JIMMY *and* ELLIOTT *begin to tiptoe toward the couch.* FRANKLIN JR., *though his back is to both of them, senses that he is about to be attacked*)

FRANKLIN JR. You leave me alone. (ELLIOTT *and* JIMMY *rush* FRANKLIN JR. *and wrestle him off the couch.* FRANKLIN JR. *calls out*) That's a rotten thing to do. (*He is now on the floor, and repeats earnestly*) A real rotten thing to do.

(ELEANOR *appears from the study door*)

ELEANOR Hello, Jimmy—Elliott.

JIMMY Mother, you missed the real fun. We finished up swimming—

ELEANOR Anna told me all about it.

ELLIOTT It was freezing—absolutely freezing.

(*The boys begin picking up their suits and towels*)

ELEANOR Where's Johnny?

JIMMY He's with Father on the dock. (ELEANOR *crosses over to a cardboard megaphone that hangs near the door.* JIMMY *calls out with mock alarm*) Oh, no, Mother.

ELEANOR It's time they were home. (ELLIOTT *and* FRANKLIN JR., *off to a side, are silently hand-wrestling, unperceived by* ELEANOR, *who crosses to the screen door, opens it and calls out*) Franklin! Johnny! (*Then, even louder*) Franklin! Johnny!!

JIMMY Mother, I hate to say this, but your voice coming through there sounds like the call to judgment.

ELEANOR That's enough from you, Mr. James Roosevelt. Now, upstairs. All of you—upstairs.

(*She points her finger to the upper floor. The boys nod and then form a group. They hide their right fists behind their backs and then, at a nod of* JIMMY'S *head, extend their hands with fingers outstretched. After they do this,* JIMMY *and* ELLIOTT *appear to be disgusted*)

FRANKLIN JR. (*Preening*) This time I win.

ELEANOR (*Smiles at them and then turns to the door and lifts up her megaphone and calls*) Franklin! Johnny!

(JIMMY *and* ELLIOTT *make a seat for* FRANKLIN JR. *with their hands, and then carry him up the steps, groaning loudly at his weight*)

ELLIOTT (*As they go up*) He's stuffed with lead—all lead.

(ELEANOR *hangs up the megaphone as* EDWARD *enters with a slip of paper and pencil. He is a young colored man, about twenty*)

EDWARD Mrs. McGowan says she needs all this from town, Mrs. Roosevelt.

(ELEANOR *takes the list and studies it*)

ELEANOR (*Nodding*) We'll pick up everything tomorrow, Edward. (*She returns the list to* EDWARD) And please add some hard candy and chocolate. Also, some cigarettes for Mr. Roosevelt.

(EDWARD *nods as he makes a notation.* ANNA, *now dressed in casual clothes, comes down the steps. She carries a book*)

ANNA Mother, I don't know why you picked *Julius Caesar* for us to read tonight. All the good parts are for men.

ELEANOR You and I, like all the others, will double up in the parts.

ANNA I'd like to read Brutus.

ELEANOR Your father makes the final decisions on casting. (*She turns to* EDWARD) Please tell Mrs. McGowan that we're going sailing and picnicking again tomorrow. I'll talk with her later about the lunch.

EDWARD Yes, Mrs. Roosevelt. (*He exits*)

ANNA Mother, we'd all appreciate it if we could get something other than fried chicken and hard-boiled eggs.

ELEANOR (*She nods her head*) Then tomorrow perhaps we'll try fried eggs and hard-boiled chicken.

(ANNA *looks at her, aghast. Glimpsed coming up the porch is* FDR. *He is about forty at this time, muscular, tall and graceful. He is wearing a white cap, a bathing suit and a robe*)

FDR (*Calling from porch*) Eleanor, they heard you all the way across to Eastport.

ELEANOR (*To* ANNA) Stand by, the Captain's home.

(FDR *opens the door*)

FDR Hello, Eleanor. Sis. (*To someone offstage*) Come on, small fry.

(FDR *lifts* JOHNNY *through the bay window and into the room*)

ANNA Last again—the runt.

JOHNNY Don't call me runt. I'm Johnny.

FDR (*Rumpling* JOHNNY's *hair*) You tell her, son. Eleanor, you missed all the fun.

ELEANOR (*Wearily*) So Anna, James, Elliott and Franklin Jr. have told me.

(MARIE *enters from upstairs*)

MARIE Ah, there you are, my friend Johnny.

JOHNNY Marie, I don't want to go upstairs.

ELEANOR Yes you do.

JOHNNY (*To* FDR, *who has crossed to the couch*) Father?

(FDR *shakes his head*)

MARIE Johnny, *il faut t'habiller pour diner.*

JOHNNY *Un moment, s'il vous plait.* Papa, *comment va tu?*

FDR *Ca va bien.* Come on, I'll make your journey upstairs a pleasant one.

(FDR *sweeps* JOHNNY *up on his back and races up the steps with him*)

JOHNNY Giddyup-giddyap.

MARIE *Voila,* Johnny! Dinner as usual, Mrs. Roosevelt?

(*She starts up the stairs*)

ELEANOR Yes, Marie. Six-thirty.

(*We hear the voices of the boys as they greet their father as he arrives upstairs with* JOHNNY *on his back*)

JIMMY'S VOICE Hello, Father. Why don't you do that for me?

ELLIOTT'S VOICE I don't want to read Cassius.

FRANKLIN JR.'S VOICE I don't think I like Shakespeare at all.

ANNA (*To* ELEANOR, *as she hears the loud voices*) Boys are so loud and noisy. Mother, how you put up with the four of them. I don't know.

ELEANOR The four boys are easy. (*She points to* ANNA) It's the one girl.

ANNA (*Rather proud*) Do you think I'm difficult?

ELEANOR I think you feel surrounded by the men in the family.

ANNA (*Not at all perturbed*) Before Granny went to Europe she told me she thinks you're too severe with me.

ELEANOR I'm aware of your chats with Granny.

ANNA (*Confidentially*) Actually, Granny spoils us. The boys can talk her out of anything—all they have to do is speak a little French or agree with her.

ELEANOR And what about you?

ANNA Oh, of course, so can I.

(FDR *has just started down the stairs*)

FDR (*To* ANNA) So can you what?

ANNA (*Puzzled*) What?

FDR I heard you say "so can I."

ANNA Oh—talk Granny out of anything I want—just like the boys. Especially if I agree with her when she says something about Mr. Howe.

(JIMMY *comes down dressed. He carries a copy of* Julius Caesar)

JIMMY Oh, Father, is Mr. Howe coming back here?

FDR No. He's going to be tied up in Washington.

ELEANOR (*Suspiciously*) Jimmy, why do you ask?

JIMMY Nothing.

FDR Why do you ask—nothing? What kind of English is that? (*Then slowly, looking at* JIMMY) Why do you ask?

JIMMY For no reason.

FDR That's better.

ELEANOR But you had a reason, Jimmy. I want you to tell me.

JIMMY Well, usually he rooms next to me, and that coughing and—(*He illustrates, wheezes*) wheezing he does so much keeps me up at night. And if he burns that incense to stop the coughing—that's worse than anything.

FDR You never appear to be suffering from a lack of sleep.

JIMMY Father, I'm serious—

FDR (*Cutting in*) Jimmy—I'm serious, too. I want no criticism of or complaints about Mr. Louie Howe from you or anyone else. Is that understood?

JIMMY Understood.

ANNA Granny always says that Mr. Howe—

FDR (*Cutting in*) I know all about Granny's opinions of Mr. Howe and I don't want them repeated by you. (*Then, closing the door to discussion*) And I would appreciate it if you and Jimmy would do some rehearsing for tonight's reading. (*He indicates the side door.* JIMMY *and* ANNA *know when to answer back and when not to. They go out the side door.* FDR *looks up at* ELEANOR) Babs, how about a hard drink? I feel rather tired and achy. That's the first swim I've had in years that didn't refresh me.

ELEANOR You should be more careful.

FDR Eleanor, I am not catching another cold and I am not becoming an alcoholic.

ELEANOR I just want you to get out of that wet suit.

FDR In a few minutes. (ELEANOR *goes to the cabinet underneath the stairway and prepares* FDR'S *drink.* FDR *glances at a newspaper*) It's a pleasure to open a paper and see my name out of it. This is a tidy item. Almost six million unemployed and Harding playing his tuba. (*He tosses his cap on the window seat and walks toward the couch.* ELEANOR *hands him a drink*) Thanks, Babs. Good—that will take the chill out of my bones. (*He refers again to the paper*) I often think of something Woodrow Wilson said to me. "It is only once in a generation that a people can be lifted above material things. That is why conservative government is in the saddle for two-thirds of the time."

ELEANOR Louie insists that you can reverse the trend.

FDR Yes, I know. He doesn't like my staying in this Wall Street job. Says it's hardly the place for a dedicated progressive.

ELEANOR Well, Franklin, is it?

FDR Babs, it's five hundred a week. And confidentially, Mrs. R., the light on my political horizon appears rather dim and dark. There is nothing as unattractive to a party as a defeated candidate.

ELEANOR I hardly think you will be held responsible for the defeat of the Democratic Party. After all, Cox was the presidential candidate, not you.

FDR Babs, I've weathered battles with Tammany Hall, seven years in the Navy Department, and Ma*ma*'s massive objections to politics—which she rates one step higher than garbage collecting. I am quite sure that Wall Street will not corrupt my political convictions.

ELEANOR That's a comfort.

(FDR *goes toward her, teasingly*)

FDR Babs, if I get into deep water, keep an eye on me.

ELEANOR "God takes man into deep water not to drown him but to cleanse him."

FDR Helpful hint from helpful wife. Thank you, ma'am Thank you kindly.

(ELLIOTT *and* FRANKLIN JR. *come downstairs*)

ELLIOTT Ma, we're hungry.

ELEANOR It'll only be a few moments now.

FDR (*Picking up a letter*) From Ma*ma*.

FRANKLIN JR. What does Granny say?

(ANNA *and* JIMMY *come in from the side room*)

ANNA Father, we have to decide about who's going to read what.

(JOHNNY *comes down the steps, followed by* MARIE)

FDR As you know, we'll all have to play a variety of roles. However, the main assignments are as follows: Your mother will read Calpurnia—Anna, you shall read Portia—(*He eyes her*) And Cinna the Poet, and Octavius. You, Jimmy, shall be Brutus.

JIMMY I've been studying Antony.

FDR I shall read Marc Antony. You are Brutus. Elliott, you will make a fine Cassius. You, Franklin, have the round look of Casca. And you, Johnny, will be the mobs, the citizens and the sounds of battle. (JOHNNY *nods, pleased*) And you, Marie, you will be Julius Caesar.

MARIE *Merci.*

(FDR *looks archly at the others*)

FDR Probably my greatest stroke of casting.

ELLIOTT What's in Granny's letter?

ANNA Please tell us, Father.

(FDR *picks up the letter from Mama*)

FDR Well, let's see. Granny has moved to London to see Cousin Muriel, whose slight operation apparently was successful. Though Ma*ma* doesn't have a high opinion of British medicine. (*He laughs, then reads silently a moment*) Granny doesn't approve of Muriel's bed. Too hard.

JIMMY She says my bed's too soft.

FDR Granny believes in hard beds for men—soft beds for women. (*He resumes reading*) Now—Granny may sail on the twenty-fourth, which would get her home on the thirty-first—or maybe a week later, which would bring her home September the seventh. (*He laughs*) She may stay. She loves the hotel. "Much love to the precious children. I expect to find a French family on my return. Devotedly, Mama." (*He puts the letter down and looks at the children*) That means Granny expects you all to be speaking perfect French. (*He continues to look at them*) So you had better be speaking perfect French. *Ici on parle français.*

(EDWARD *now enters*)

EDWARD Mrs. Roosevelt, dinner's ready.

ELEANOR Thank you, Edward.

ELLIOTT What has Mrs. McGowan got to eat tonight?

ELEANOR Whatever Mrs. McGowan has to eat you will enjoy.

ELLIOTT I'm sure of that, Mother. I just wanted to know.

ELEANOR Let life surprise you, Elliott. It's more fun that way.

JIMMY (*Sitting down next to* FDR) How's your arm, Father?

ELEANOR (*Protesting*) Franklin.

FDR This will only take a minute, Babs. (*He puts his arm on the table opposite* JIMMY. *They clasp hands. The children group around.* JIMMY *is already straining every muscle*) Ready?

JIMMY Ready.

(FDR puts JIMMY'S *arm down, rolling him to the floor at the same time*)

FDR Undefeated and still champion. (*The children cheer and move out toward the dining room.* FDR *saunters over to the bay window*) This time of day is always the best. It's as if the sun were standing still for a last glimpse—a long lingering look before saying good night.

ELEANOR It's a nice quiet time.

FDR I wish I could stay till after Labor Day.

(*Suddenly* FDR *stumbles and grabs his back. He recovers.* ELEANOR *sees the grimace of pain and crosses to him*)

ELEANOR Why, Franklin!

FDR Must be a spot of lumbago—(ELEANOR *puts her hand to his brow*) No, I don't feel feverish. Just suddenly—(*He snaps his fingers*) Like that—

ELEANOR You get into bed. I'll bring you a tray.

FDR (*Half a smile*) I hoped you'd say that.

(ELEANOR *goes toward the kitchen. Just as* FDR *hits the steps, the sound of the children in the dining room can be heard. Both* ELEANOR *and* FDR *stop as we hear the voices of the children, offstage*)

VOICES Two!—Four!—Six!—Eight!—Who do we appreciate?
—Mrs. McGowan! Mrs. McGowan! Mrs. McGowan! Yaaay!

(*Sounds of handclapping and yells.* ELEANOR *exits.* FDR, *amused, pauses and listens, then continues slowly up the steps, as*

The Curtain Falls

Scene Two

Scene: The scene is the same. It is September 1, 1921. It is night. The kerosene lights dimly illuminate the room.

At rise: LOUIS HOWE *enters from the kitchen with a tray covered with a white napkin. He is a small and homely man. He wears, as he does at all times, a badly wrinkled suit and vest, along with a high stiff collar. His ties and handkerchiefs are garish. He is a chain smoker and an asthmatic. He is never without a cigarette in his mouth or in his hand. He hurries upstairs.*

ELEANOR'S VOICE (*Offstage*) Louie—

HOWE Be right there.

ELEANOR'S VOICE (*Offstage*) Thank you, Louie.

HOWE Call me if you need anything. (*He comes down the steps and sees* JIMMY. *During the above,* JIMMY *has crossed to the bottom of the stairs, wearing pajamas and bathrobe*) Hello, Jim. What's wrong?

JIMMY Nothing, Mr. Howe.

HOWE Then why aren't you asleep?

JIMMY I couldn't sleep. How's my father?

HOWE Having a fairly good night.

JIMMY Can I see him tonight?

HOWE No—in a couple of days.

JIMMY We're all a little scared.

HOWE (*In a reprimanding tone*) Well your father isn't, and he wouldn't want you to be, Jim.

JIMMY I'll try. I'd feel better if I knew what was going on, but I don't want to bother Mother.

HOWE That's right. She's had enough to do for the past three weeks.

JIMMY But—

HOWE But what?

JIMMY Sometimes I get frightened. So does Anna.

HOWE Well, stop being frightened. Those germs never ran into anybody as tough as your father. They'll be yelling for help by the time he gets through with them.

JIMMY He's strong, all right.

HOWE (*Now placatingly*) He's a strong and big man in many ways. Jimmy, when I first got up here I was scared, too. I was worried about your father being so sick. But now he's beginning to fight back—and when he fights—well, sir, you know the first time I saw him was in Albany in nineteen eleven. He was fighting a tough battle with Tammany Hall. Believe me, they can fight like roughnecks. Well, he won that one going away—like what Dempsey did to Carpentier. And, Jimmy, he's going to win this one.

JIMMY (*Relieved*) I hope you're right.

HOWE I've never been wrong in my life. Only once, when I figured the ice on the pond in Saratoga was thick enough to skate on. Well, sir, it took three days to wring me out.

(ELEANOR, *carrying a tray, appears on the stairs.* JIMMY *and* HOWE *turn as she appears*)

ELEANOR (*As she sees* JIMMY) Jimmy.

JIMMY I was just up for a glass of water, Mother.

(JIMMY *takes the tray and exits to the kitchen*)

HOWE All right?

(ELEANOR *nods as she takes off her apron.* JIMMY *returns from the kitchen*)

ELEANOR All right, dear. Now you go in and get some sleep.

JIMMY I will. And you'd better get some rest, too, Mother. (ELEANOR *nods*) 'Night.

ELEANOR Good night, James.

JIMMY Good night, Mr. Howe.

(JIMMY *exits into the side room*)

HOWE Eleanor, why the hell can't we get some electric lights in here?

ELEANOR You know we can't. Louie, what's bothering you?

HOWE Where's Mrs. Roosevelt?

ELEANOR Ma*ma*'s in her room. She'll probably be down in a few minutes. Louie, be understanding. It's been a desperately unhappy day for her.

HOWE I am understanding, Eleanor. I like the old lady. She fascinates me. Monumental and impregnable as the Rock of Gibraltar.

ELEANOR I know the problem that you have with Ma*ma*.

HOWE It's no problem. She just hates the sight of me. She considers me the ward-heeler in Franklin's life.

ELEANOR Louie, don't quarrel with her.

HOWE Eleanor—I promise to shinny on my side if she shinnies on hers. (*A pause*) It's going to be rough, but you're going to have to tell her the truth.

ELEANOR (*Wearily*) Louie, if we can only get him well enough to move him into New York. Each day with him here is like—(*Controlling herself*) He should be in a hospital, getting the best care, the most modern treatment.

HOWE Now you just remember this—nobody could have done more than you, or done it better.

(*At this moment,* MRS. SARA DELANO ROOSEVELT *comes down the steps. At this time she is in her middle sixties, a strong, dominant, vibrant figure of a woman. She is dressed in expensive and elegant clothes. She is at all times the Lady of the Manor. She guards her emotions in stoical form. While everyone knows exactly what she thinks, the only one she ever quarrels with openly and nakedly is* FDR)

SARA Eleanor? Franklin sleeping?

ELEANOR Yes—he's been resting for over two hours.

SARA Has the pain eased?

ELEANOR A bit. His legs are less sensitive to touch. A cup of tea, Ma*ma?*

SARA I would like a cup.

ELEANOR It will only be a moment, dear.

(*As* ELEANOR *exits,* SARA *recognizes the presence of* HOWE. *He puts his suit jacket on. Aware that he is now permitted to speak, he does so*)

HOWE How are you feeling, Mrs. Roosevelt?

SARA Oh, Mr. Howe. A little tired—but a good night's rest will pick me up, I'm sure. I came directly from New York after the boat docked. The crossing was rather rough—and seemed endless.

HOWE Yes, so Eleanor said.

SARA How is your wife?

HOWE Why. Grace is fine, thank you. She took my son Hartley home with her yesterday.

(SARA *nods, then takes note of the smoky atmosphere*)

SARA The air is rather stuffy, don't you think?

HOWE (*Casually*) We had the door open, but it's damn cold outside.

SARA (*After a polite pause*) Have you been here all the time since Franklin's illness?

HOWE I arrived a couple of days after he took ill. Been here since—and plan to stay till we take him back.

SARA Do the doctors know when that will be?

HOWE They hope in a couple of weeks.

SARA I admire the way all of you are behaving. (ELEANOR *has entered with the tea; she places it before* SARA. *To* ELEANOR) Thank you, dear.

ELEANOR Louie—tea?

HOWE No, thanks.

SARA Eleanor dear, if you're not too worn out—I'm so anxious to hear as much as I can about everything.

ELEANOR Yes, Ma*ma.*

HOWE Mrs. Roosevelt, this girl has worked like a squad of trained nurses. Dr. Lovett was amazed at how well she had done it all.

SARA (*To* ELEANOR) Couldn't you get any nurses, dear?

ELEANOR We tried, but none were available. Campobello is quite remote.

SARA If you don't mind—this is the first opportunity we've had to talk.

ELEANOR Of course, Ma*ma*. Franklin was taken ill on August tenth—just three weeks ago. At first it seemed to be a heavy cold. Finally Dr. Bennet called in a specialist, who diagnosed it as a clot on the spinal cord.

SARA He couldn't have been a good specialist.

ELEANOR We thought he was. But Franklin didn't respond to the treatment. About a week ago Uncle Fred reached me by telephone—we have to go into town for that.

SARA I always thought it was absurd to be so cut off.

ELEANOR You know that Franklin never wanted a phone here.

SARA Go ahead, dear.

ELEANOR Uncle Fred had talked to some other doctors, who began to suspect it was infantile paralysis. So he arranged for Dr. Lovett of Boston to come up. He diagnosed it almost immediately. And we're doing as he suggested ever since.

SARA And what does he think—how severe is the paralysis?

ELEANOR He believes it to be a mild attack—and feels that Franklin will recover almost completely.

SARA (*Slowly*) Almost?—

ELEANOR Well, Ma*ma*—at first Franklin lost control even of his hands. He couldn't write—or hold a spoon. Now his arms and hands are almost all well. We still don't know about his legs—or—his back.

SARA (*Slowly*) He can't sit up?

ELEANOR No, dear, not yet.

(SARA *puts down her cup, takes a handkerchief and puts it to her lips, stifling a desire to cry*)

HOWE The doctors feel sure his back muscles will be all right.

SARA His legs—those wonderful legs—what about them?

ELEANOR The doctors don't know.

SARA (*Shaking her head*) It's too much—I can't believe it. (*Sobbing*) My poor boy—my poor boy—

ELEANOR Ma*ma*—perhaps we shouldn't talk any more—you're exhausted.

SARA (*Stopping her tears*) No—I couldn't sleep right now. The children? Is it safe for them to be here?

ELEANOR Dr. Lovett said having already been exposed to the illness there is no point moving them.

SARA I can certainly help with the children.

ELEANOR That would be wonderful.

(*She passes her hand over her tired eyes*)

HOWE (*Seeing the gesture*) Eleanor—you have to get some rest. We all do. (*Seeing that no one picks up the hint*) I think I'll turn in myself. Will you excuse me?

SARA Good night, Mr. Howe.

ELEANOR Rest well, Louie.

HOWE 'Night. (*He exits up steps—wheezing and coughing and smoking. Suddenly he trips on the dimly lit steps*) I don't know why the hell they can't put some electric lights in here.

(HOWE *is out of sight*)

SARA (*After a pause*) He's a vulgar little man.

ELEANOR He's a very dear little man.

SARA I find him very difficult.

ELEANOR You make that quite clear.

SARA I'm not skillful at hiding my true feelings, Eleanor.

ELEANOR That may not be a virtue, Ma*ma.* You should know as soon as Louie heard of Franklin's illness, he gave up a lucrative job in Washington to rush here and help out. There's nothing in life more important to him than Franklin.

SARA Nor to any of us.

ELEANOR Then, that's something we can share with Louie, isn't it?

SARA (*A weary sigh*) It has been a grueling day. I'm tired.

ELEANOR Ma*ma,* there's something very special in the relationship between Louie and Franklin.

SARA I've never quite understood it. It's possible Mr. Howe merely enjoys riding along on Franklin's coattails.

(HOWE *has been coming down the steps and has heard* SARA'S *last remark. He covers his anger*)

HOWE Eleanor—

ELEANOR (*Quickly rising*) Yes, Louie?

HOWE Franklin needs you a minute.

(ELEANOR *goes up the steps quickly*)

SARA Eleanor!

HOWE It's nothing alarming, Mrs. Roosevelt.

SARA (*Determined to be polite*) You suffer a great deal from asthma, don't you?

HOWE (*As he lights a cigarette*) A great deal. I'd be lonesome without it.

SARA You know that smoking isn't very good for you—you know that.

HOWE I do.

(*He puffs deliberately in defiance of* SARA'S *advice*)

SARA What are the plans for Franklin after they take him to New York?

HOWE First he goes to the hospital—and then, well, I guess it depends on how all that goes.

SARA You say that he will be able to be moved in two or three weeks.

HOWE We hope so.

SARA As soon as he's able to leave the hospital I want him to go to Hyde Park. Everything he loves is there. It's home to him. Always has been. It's large enough for the entire family and that's where he can be made most comfortable.

HOWE Well, I'm sure that as soon as Franklin's well enough he and Eleanor will decide where he would like to recuperate.

SARA If Franklin's to have any permanent injury, the best place for him is Hyde Park. We can make a full life for him there. He can write, take care of the estate, raise his family as he was raised, and there will be enough to keep him active without overtaxing him or spending his energy.

HOWE Mrs. Roosevelt, I've heard Franklin say that in public service a man must be prepared to spend and be spent. He may not be willing to accept a sedentary life in the country.

SARA Mr. Howe, we must do everything that is possible to discourage him from remaining active in politics.

HOWE Mrs. Roosevelt, Hyde Park or Timbuktu, Franklin's political future is ordained. That sounds mystical, I know. But I feel it as sure as I feel my heart beating.

SARA (*The politeness is wearing thin*) Believe me, Mr. Howe, I respect your devotion, but Franklin is more to me than a prospective candidate for public office. He's my son.

HOWE He is also Eleanor's husband, the father of five children and my dearest friend.

SARA (*The hard fist*) Then he is blessed indeed to be the subject of so much affection.

HOWE (*Losing his temper*) But he is, above all, himself, Mrs. Roosevelt, and he happens to be the best damned progressive in the country.

SARA (*Closing the iron door*) My only interest is in his getting well—not his status as a politician. I am grateful for the care and devotion you have given Franklin. I am less grateful for your untimely and grandiose schemes.

HOWE Mrs. Roosevelt, for the next few months Franklin may have need for some grandiose schemes. So may we all.

(SARA *gives him a cold and penetrating glance*)

SARA Good night, Mr. Howe.

(*She turns and walks up the steps as*

The Curtain Falls

Scene Three

Scene: We are in the living room again. There is some luggage stacked around. It is a sunny morning, September 13, 1921.

At rise: MISSY LEHAND *is stage right, typing from some notes. She is* FDR's *private secretary. She is a handsome woman, with auburn hair and a strong and sure manner.* EDWARD *comes into the living room and takes out some of the baggage.* JOHNNY, *carrying a bow and arrow and wearing a simple Indian headdress, follows behind* EDWARD. *As he comes in, he lets out an Indian war whoop.*

EDWARD Mr. Johnny, I'm busy. I can't play Indians any more.

JOHNNY Let me help you carry the bags.

EDWARD It's not your work. Now you go about your business and let me go about mine.

(EDWARD *now has three of the suitcases and out he goes*)

MISSY How, Big Chief! Need anything?

JOHNNY Just Anna. Jimmy sent me in for her. He orders us around like we were in the Navy. (*Calling out*) Anna!

MISSY Ssh.

JOHNNY (*In a hoarse whisper*) Sorry. Anna!

ANNA (*From upstairs*) Ssh. (*She appears, holding her suitcase. She is dressed for departure*) Stop yelling like a wild Indian.

JOHNNY Jimmy says—

ANNA What Jimmy says doesn't interest me in the slightest.

JOHNNY We're supposed to wait outside.

ANNA I know—like—children.

JOHNNY I enjoy being a boy.

ANNA I'm going to have some breakfast and go out the back way.

(*She exits to kitchen*)

JOHNNY Miss LeHand, are they gonna carry Father out on a stretcher?

MISSY Well, that's the plan.

JOHNNY Why can't Jimmy, Elliott, Franklin and I do it?

MISSY (*Smiling, but sensitive to* JOHNNY's *ambitions*) That's a wonderful idea. But, you see, your father has made other plans, and it's too late to change.

(LOUIE HOWE, *carrying a suitcase, comes down the steps from above*)

JOHNNY Okay. I'd better go before Jimmy sends Elliott for me. (*He looks at* HOWE) Good morning, Mr. Howe.

(HOWE *waves an airy good morning.* JOHNNY *exits*)

MISSY He's a cute one.

HOWE They're all cute. But there sure are a helluva lot of them. How's it going, Missy?

MISSY Now that Anna is downstairs, the kids are all packed and waiting for the Robert E. Lee.

HOWE Ma*ma?*

MISSY Upstairs with the Boss and Mrs. R. Doc Bennet, too.

HOWE We've got about a half an hour.

MISSY This is going to be a rough trip for Mr. R.

HOWE Once we get him across the bay and into Eastport—the rough time's over.

MISSY (*Putting papers into a briefcase*) You're going to have a lot of angry newspapermen breathing down your collar. They all want to see Mr. R.

HOWE They'll see him—after he's on the train all propped up in his berth—a grin on his face. Once we get to Eastport—I'll flash the other dock, tell the newspapermen to come over, and explain there was a change of plans due to the tide or currents or something.

MISSY (*Glancing at some notes before she packs them*) When do we break the news that the Boss has infantile?

HOWE Later. When we get to New York. Some time tomorrow. (*Reading from a release*) "After thorough examinations, doctors today revealed Franklin D. Roosevelt recently suffered a mild attack of infantile paralysis. His legs have been temporarily affected, but it is anticipated he will have a complete recovery."

MISSY (*Glumly*) Well, that's a gay little news item.

HOWE Missy—where are those usual radiantly hopeful thoughts?

MISSY Louie—I've been here for two weeks taking dictation and trying to act as he does—as if nothing is the matter. Sometimes it seems a sad and foolish game. He lies there, rattling on with plans for business conferences and meetings. Overhaul the Democratic Party—select the candidates for twenty-two and twenty-four—organize this charity and reorganize that. I listen with wonder and I want to cry.

HOWE Missy—maybe he doesn't mean one word of what he's planning or trying to do—but he wants us to believe it—so, Missy, believe. (EDWARD *enters*) Edward, my stuff goes into the boat headed to Eastport.

EDWARD Yes sir, I know. (*Turns to* MISSY) What about your things, Miss LeHand?

MISSY To the first boat. Thanks.

(EDWARD *by now has the next to the last load, and exits. As he starts out,* DR. BENNET *comes down from upstairs*)

BENNET Our patient's about ready to be moved. I'll send the men in with the stretcher. When they bring Mr. Roosevelt down, we'll give him a short rest in here and then take him to the boat.

MISSY Doctor—

BENNET Yes?

MISSY How is he today?

BENNET About the same. He's in pain, but I've given him something to help that. He's running a fever—but he refuses to take it seriously. Body of a bull—disposition of a lamb.

(*He crosses to the door and goes out to the porch as* SARA *comes in. She is dressed for travel*)

HOWE Good morning, Mrs. Roosevelt.

SARA Good morning. Are the children all ready, Miss LeHand?

MISSY Yes, they're all outside.

SARA I don't think they should see their father carried on a stretcher.

HOWE Well—I'm afraid that will be unavoidable.

MISSY Certainly the least excitement for Mr. Roosevelt, the better.

(EDWARD *returns for the last few pieces of luggage.* DR. BENNET *and four men enter. The men are villagers and are dressed in dungarees, sweaters and clothing typical of coastal towns. They are neighbors and friends. The stretcher they carry is homemade, crude but serviceable*)

HOWE Good morning, men.

FRANKLIN CALDER (*The leader of the group*) Morning. (*Glancing at* SARA *and* MISSY) Ma'am. Ma'am.

SARA Good morning, Captain.

(*The others nod as they remove their hats*)

MISSY Morning.

HOWE I want to thank all of you sincerely for what you have done and are doing.

CALDER No thanks expected, Mr. Howe.

BENNET Look at the stretcher they made. They've even fixed up a back rest.

HOWE Wonderful—really.

(*The men nod their acknowledgment of* HOWE'S *compliment*)

BENNET We'd better move.

(*As the men are directed upstairs by* DR. BENNET, *who precedes them,* EDWARD *exits.* SARA *looks upstairs apprehensively.* HOWE *is sympathetic to her feelings.* ELEANOR *comes down from upstairs. She carries her large handbag, an extra blanket, and a soft felt hat of* FDR's. *She is tired, and, like the others, tense but contained*)

MEN (*Passing* ELEANOR) Good morning, ma'am.

ELEANOR Good morning. Good morning, Captain Calder. (*Handing* MISSY *an envelope*) Missy—these are some get-well letters which came in before you arrived. I've had no time to answer.

MISSY (*With a smile*) Small wonder.

(*She puts the envelope in her briefcase*)

ELEANOR (*Turns to* MISSY) Are the children all ready?

MISSY Yes. Mademoiselle is with them—near the dock.

SARA Do you think the children should see this?

ELEANOR They may have to learn to see a lot of things.

SARA Perhaps. But it may be a shock, particularly to the younger ones.

HOWE They'll get older.

SARA (*To* HOWE, *shocked*) Mr. Howe.

HOWE I didn't mean that the way it sounded. But I think Eleanor's right.

SARA I believe you and I have varying opinions of what is right and wrong.

ELEANOR Frankly, I suppose the children are excited by it. They'd probably love to be carried to a boat on a stretcher.

SARA Furthermore, Franklin's arrival at Eastport should not be handled as a circus.

ELEANOR Ma*ma,* Franklin is a man of some reputation. We can't give an imperial order and ask the crowds to disperse.

HOWE I think you must agree, Mrs. Roosevelt, that it is far better to have the ubiquitous press first find Franklin sitting in his berth in the train, rather than see him carried on a stretcher.

SARA Franklin's day of departure could have been kept secret.

HOWE No, it could not, Mrs. Roosevelt. The newspapermen have been eying Campobello since the day Franklin took ill.

(SARA's *eyes go to the stair landing*)

ELEANOR (*Crossing to* SARA) Ma*ma,* I too have seen him walk up and down those steps many times.

SARA I do not approve of Franklin being placed on exhibition.

ELEANOR This is not a pleasant time for any of us—particularly Franklin.

(*As* SARA *considers this, the stretcher appears, borne by the four men.* DR. BENNET *guides the men. On the stretcher is* FDR. *He wears a plain dark-blue robe over pajamas and is partly covered by blankets*)

BENNET (*Instructing*) Lift your side—right—that's it. Lower the other side. That's fine. Over the post—

FDR Men, it's a lot easier going down than up. Be grateful for small favors. (SARA, ELEANOR, HOWE *and* MISSY *watch. Their emotions, of course, are guarded, but we sense by their tenseness and reaction what they feel.* SARA *grips her pocketbook,* MISSY *stands tense, and* ELEANOR, *holding the brim of* FDR's *hat, fingers it nervously. The men bring the stretcher down safely and set it on the floor. It is clear* FDR *is still a sick man but trying to cover his condition by good humor*) Thank you, gentlemen. The journey was a pleasant one. Where's my missus?

ELEANOR Here, darling.

FDR How about a look around, Doc?

BENNET Yes indeed.

(*With* ELEANOR *and* FRANKLIN CALDER, DR. BENNET *props the back of the stretcher up so that* FDR, *sitting up, can look around. By now, the others in the room are relaxed and cover their nervousness.* DR. BENNET *ushers the men out, indicating that he will call them when ready*)

FDR I tell you there's no other way to travel. (*He digs into his robe, produces a pack of cigarettes and his holder. He peers around*) The place hasn't changed in the month I've been away. (HOWE, *stepping over to him, lights the cigarette for* FDR) Thanks, Louie, my boy. How have you planned the logistics?

HOWE (*Knowing* FDR *loves these shenanigans*) First, the children, Missy, your mother and Eleanor take off for the main dock. That's where the sightseers and the press have congregated. A goodly crowd has gathered and waits eagerly. (*Going into a heavy Dutch burlesque accent*) But, *mein herr,* vhile all der peepuls is vatching da von boat coming on der vater—vee go avay in da odder boat for Eastport und get on der train. *Gut? Nicht wahr?*

FDR Ah, a diversionary tactic.

HOWE Precisely, *mein herr.*

FDR As Assistant Secretary of the Navy I used to rate a seventeen-gun salute. Have you arranged for that?

HOWE You're just an ex-assistant—no guns. You're lucky we got water.

FDR Eleanor, you'd better give me that hat before you tear it to ribbons. (ELEANOR *hands him his hat, which he puts on his head*) How do I look—snappy?

SARA Never better.

FDR Louie, I approve of your plan.

HOWE It's about time. I've been waiting breathlessly.

FDR (*To the others*) He's not fooling. Louie's first love was the theatre. He loves applause.

(LOUIE *executes a neat time-step. The others, in the spirit of it, applaud*)

HOWE (*Looks at his watch*) I hate to break up the party but I think it's about time boat number one got on its way.

MISSY That's me.

FDR Missy, plan on coming to the hospital Thursday morning. Will you have everything typed by then?

MISSY Of course.

FDR Fine. What's the date of that Boy Scout dinner?

MISSY The seventh of November.

FDR We'd better cancel that. I don't know if I'll feel up to making speeches until after the New Year.

(MISSY *nods as she makes notes*)

MISSY Right.

FDR And bring that list of conferences I've had to cancel out because of this ridiculous child's disease, and we'll plan some new dates.

BENNET That's all, Franklin. They have to get started. You can do all that on the train.

SARA We'll be on the way before they bring you out?

FDR I expect so, Ma*ma*.

SARA I'll tell the children that they'll see you on the train.
(SARA *gives* ELEANOR *a half-glance.* FDR *isn't aware of this by-play, but* HOWE *is, as is* MISSY)

FDR Bon voyage!

SARA (*Gives him a kiss*) Bon voyage!

MISSY See you, Boss.
(FDR *waves a farewell as* SARA *and* MISSY *leave*)

FDR The party is thinning out. (*He removes his hat and rubs his hand through his hair absently*) I think I can say the same for my hair. Where's Duffy?

ELEANOR Outside, waiting for us.

FDR Please bring him in, Babs. Let him ride with me.

BENNET There's no harm in it. I'll get him.
(*He exits and* ELEANOR *follows him to the doorway*)

FDR Well, Louie, I must say you look wretched.

HOWE You know how I hate sea travel.

FDR You could get rid of your asthma if you'd breathe in some good sea air and cut out those cigarettes.

HOWE Look who the hell's talking about cigarettes.

FDR I haven't got asthma.

HOWE *Touché!*

(BENNET *arrives with* DUFFY, *a black Scottie, and* ELEANOR *carries him in and hands him to* FDR)

FDR Hello, Duffy, you old pirate. Say, you're getting fat. One of these days I'll have to take you for a long run in the woods.

(*There is a pause. Does* FDR *mean it? Does he think he will be able to? We don't know. Now* EDWARD *enters*)

EDWARD We're ready to go, Mrs. Roosevelt.

BENNET It's time.

ELEANOR (*She digs into her bag for some keys*) There are the keys, Edward. Now you lock up on the return trip.

EDWARD Yes, ma'am. I'll get everything shipshape.

ELEANOR Drain the pipes.

EDWARD And board up the windows till next season.

HOWE I'll walk you to the boat, Eleanor. See you on the dock, Franklin.

(HOWE *exits*)

EDWARD Good-bye, Mr. Roosevelt—and good luck to you, sir.

FDR Thank you, Edward.

(EDWARD *leaves*)

BENNET I'll be with the men, Franklin.

(*He leaves*)

ELEANOR Franklin, I'm to cross with the children.

FDR How's the sea today?

ELEANOR Choppy.

FDR West wind?

ELEANOR That's right.

FDR Is Calder handling my boat?

ELEANOR Yes.

FDR (*Reassuring her*) He's a good man.

ELEANOR I'll call the men, dear.

(ELEANOR *walks to the door to wave the men in. As she leaves,* FDR *sags back against the stretcher. Suddenly we are aware of what a strain this has been for him. He looks weary and tired. He lowers his head and then looks up and looks around the room as a wave of memories flood his mind. His hands drop in fatigue and pain, and he releases his hat, which he has been holding. It falls out of his reach. As he attempts to retrieve it we see that he cannot move his back. His fingers stretch for it but he cannot touch it. He breathes heavily.* ELEANOR *returns and, realizing what has happened, hands him has hat.* DR. BENNET *returns with the men, and* FDR *pulls himself together*)

ELEANOR Are you sure that you can manage this trip?

FDR I'm going to make a damn good try.

(FDR *puts his hat on and puts his cigarette holder in his mouth in that familar perky fashion. He holds* DUFFY *in one arm. The men reach down and lift the stretcher*)

BENNET All right, men—

(*They start out*)

FDR Gentlemen—thank you for the sedan chair. (*As he is carried out*) By gosh—I feel like the Caliph of Bagdad.

The Curtain Falls

ACT TWO

ACT TWO

SCENE ONE

Scene: It is May, 1922. Curtain reveals the downstairs living room of the New York house on Sixty-fifth Street. Like all the Roosevelt homes, it is warm and tasteful and not at all pretentious.

At rise: FDR *is seen stage right, sitting in one of his small kitchen chairs, converted for use as a wheel chair. He is working on some stamps. On the couch is a model of a sailboat on which* FDR *has been previously working. He drops some of the stamps, then scoots his chair over to a desk on the other side of the room. He picks up from the desk a gadget with an extension arm which when expanded reaches to the floor. He scoots back to the table and, using the gadget, picks up the stamps. He is already quite expert at wheeling his chair. His attitude is far from cheerful. After he works away for a moment or two,* MISSY *enters from the office next to the living room. She carries a sheaf of letters for* FDR *to sign. She, like the others who are close to* FDR, *is sensitive to his moods, and so she is aware* FDR *is having one of his rare bad days.*

MISSY Sorry, Boss, to interrupt, but you wanted to get these off. (FDR *pushes his stamps away and places the letters on the table*) I still have the letters Louie dictated—I hope to finish them before I go tonight.

(FDR *starts to read*)

MISSY In the letter to the Park Commission, I may have made a mistake. I couldn't remember whether you said *sixty* thousand trees or *sixteen.*

FDR (*Not looking up*) Six*teen.*

MISSY Good. That's what I typed in.

FDR My enunciation is usually precise enough to make the distinction between six*teen* and six*ty*.

MISSY No criticism, Mr. R. My hearing must be failing.

FDR (*Handing her a letter*) You'll have to correct this. It's *Pine*henge Farm—not *Pin*henge.

(MISSY *takes it, looks at it.* FDR *continues, referring to the next letter*) Missy, this rough draft of the letter to Cordell Hull should be triple-spaced.

MISSY (*Ruefully*) I'm having a good day.

FDR Well, if you must know, I'm having a perfectly wretched day.

MISSY I'm sorry.

FDR I can't wear the leg braces because they don't fit—and I don't know why I'm going all the way to Boston to get new ones that also won't fit. And I'm fed up with all those friendly hints that come in the mail—everything from ancient nostrums to brand new gadgets invented by people all the way from Keokuk to Zanzibar.

MISSY They all want to help—not hurt.

FDR Oh, Missy—stop it. No sweetness and light today—please. (*Refers to the letters*) Take them away.

(ELEANOR *comes in. She has been upstairs. She carries books and mail*)

ELEANOR Franklin, I've talked to Regan. He's arranged for the railroad trip to Boston.

FDR (*Almost challengingly*) I may not go to Boston.

(*He wheels over to the desk.* ELEANOR *and* MISSY *exchange a glance.* ELEANOR *gets the message*)

ELEANOR You don't have to go until Friday. You can decide by then. (*She hands the mail to* FDR) There's a cheery letter from Jimmy. And one from Woodrow Wilson.

FDR (*He is reading the letter*) I'm glad to read that Jimmy anticipates good marks. (*Reads on*) Well, that's a relief—he loves Groton. I'm sure Groton is relieved, too. (*He picks up the one from Wilson.* ELEANOR *is putting the books away.* MISSY *glances at the letters she has picked up from* FDR's *table.* FDR *reads Wilson's letter, his mood changing a bit*) It's an extremely considerate note. (*Reads*) "I am indeed delighted to hear you are getting so well, and so confidently, and I shall try and be generous enough not to envy you. I hope that your generous labors in behalf of the Wilson Foundation have not overtaxed you, and you are certainly to be congratulated on your successful leadership in the complicated and difficult undertaking." That's really quite thoughtful of him.

ELEANOR You have done a lot for the Foundation.

FDR Only because I believe in it. Either we develop some plan for world peace and order or the world will chop itself into bits.

MISSY Excuse me, Boss—may I get on with the rest of these?

FDR (*Cheerier*) On your way, Missy. Later I want to do another draft of that letter to Cordell Hull. What I've got is too obscure. (MISSY *nods and starts to exit*) Sixteen—(FDR *grins apologetically.* MISSY *understands—exits*) I was apologizing for having lost my temper.

ELEANOR I had a rather tense chore a few minutes ago. I had to let the upstairs maid go. She complained so much about all the work she had to do—most of which she never did anyway.

FDR (*Crossing to her*) Sorry, Babs. You've had a big turnover on maids this year. It's been a busy household.

ELEANOR It's been a nice household.

FDR (*Rolling his chair about the room and putting some of his things away*) I'm getting expert with this chair. It moves easily. See that. (*He executes a sharp turn*) We have to get a couple like this for Hyde Park. None of those conventional invalid wheel chairs. (*He takes another turn or two in the chair*) This exercise is stimulating—takes some of the loneliness away.

(*He crosses to the couch and picks up a sailboat*)

ELEANOR Loneliness, dear?

FDR Invalidism—(*Quickly*)—even temporary—is very lonely. I remember reading: "A sick man wishes to be where he is not." (*After a moment*) When you're forced to sit a lot—and watch others move about—you feel apart—lonely—because you can't get up and pace around. I find myself irritated when people come in here and parade all over the place. I have to keep exercising self-control to prevent screaming at them to sit down—quiet down—stand still.

ELEANOR I'll remember.

FDR You're quiet and restful.

ELEANOR (*She continues straightening out the room*) I am just tired. Is Louie in his room?

FDR He said he was going out for a feel of the pulse of the city. What he really means—he's going out to buy newspapers. Loves the Teapot Dome stories. Adores political scandals—if they embarrass Republicans.

ELEANOR (*A moment*) Franklin—are there other things I should know that you haven't told me?

FDR (*Lightly*) You mean like about Louie going out to get the papers?

ELEANOR I mean about your—loneliness.

FDR (*Not joking now*) Often when you're alone, certain fears seek you out and hunt for a place in your mind. Well, you know, I've always had a small fear about fire. Since this—(*Indicates his legs*) that fear sometimes overwhelms me. I've nightmares about being trapped and unable to move. I've been practicing crawling so I can be sure that in case of fire I could get to a window by myself—or to a door or a flight of steps.

ELEANOR I didn't know you had been—crawling.

FDR I've been trying—and I can do fairly well—by now. But soon I'll be back on my feet. The back muscles came around —and so will the legs.

ELEANOR Of course they will.

FDR (*Suddenly turns to the ship model and lifts it in one hand*) Do you like her?

ELEANOR She's lovely.

FDR She'll really sail, you know—she's not just a toy. (*He places it back on the couch*) I miss the sea. (*He wheels his chair close to* ELEANOR *and takes her hand as his words come wrenching out of him*) Eleanor, I must say this—once to someone. Those first few days at Campobello when this started, I had despair—deep, sick despair. It wasn't the pain—there was much more of that later on when they straightened the tendons in my legs. No, not the pain—it was the sense that perhaps I'd never get up again. Like a crab lying on its back. I'd look down at my fingers and exert every thought to get them to move. I'd send down orders to my legs and my toes—they didn't obey.

ELEANOR (*As he halts his speech for a moment, she goes to him, her head on his lap*) Darling—

FDR I turned to my faith, Babs—for strength to endure. I feel I have to go through this fire for some reason. Eleanor, it's a hard way to learn humility—but I've been learning by crawling. I know what is meant—you must learn to crawl before you can walk.

(*They embrace. After a moment, the front door is heard slamming and* FDR *straightens as* ANNA'S *voice is heard*)

ANNA'S VOICE Mother—Mother—Mother!

ELEANOR (*Pulls away from* FDR *and sits down, trying to compose herself*) I'm here, Anna—and do quiet down.

ANNA (*Appearing*) Oh—how are you Father?

FDR Sis—

ANNA Mother, I have to talk to you. It's important.

ELEANOR Anna, it will have to wait a little while. I have other important things.

FDR (*Starting out*) This chamber is yours, ladies. *Au revoir.*

ELEANOR (*She starts after him*) Franklin—

FDR Eleanor—I need the exercise. See you later, Sis.

(*He rolls out. After he is gone,* ELEANOR *starts to straighten up the room*)

ANNA Mother, I must talk to you.

ELEANOR Yes, dear. So you told me.

ANNA I can't talk to you on the run.

ELEANOR Anna, you can't make up all the rules. (*Continues to straighten up*) I'm listening.

ANNA It's about my room.

ELEANOR What about your room?

ANNA I cannot understand why I've been moved upstairs into a little cubbyhole—and why Mr. Howe has been given my large room—

ELEANOR That change was made weeks ago—Why has it taken you so long to question it?

ANNA Because I accepted the change without thinking of it.

ELEANOR Oh, you did?

ANNA Yes—but only yesterday—when Granny was here—she asked me the question—direct—and I could not give her a clear answer.

ELEANOR Then, Anna, I suggest you tell Granny to ask me.

(*We hear the sound of the front door being opened*)

ANNA Mother, it seems to me—

ELEANOR It seems to me you're behaving badly.

ANNA I fail to understand why Mr. Howe should—

HOWE'S VOICE (*Offstage*) Hello—

(LOUIE HOWE *enters. He is carrying a stack of newspapers*)

HOWE Ladies. May I recount the happenings on the Appian Way?

ANNA Mother, please—

ELEANOR Anna—I will not discuss this with you now.

HOWE I'm sorry. I'll go.

ANNA (*Her dignity flying high*) There's no need. Mother and I have concluded our conversation, thank you. Excuse me, please.

(*She exits*)

HOWE Marie Antoinette could not have been more noble on her way to the guillotine.

ELEANOR (*Shaking her head*) It's a busy house, Louie, very busy.

HOWE A busy world. (*Rattling through the papers*) There's an item I want you to hear, Eleanor. The Chicago *Tribune.* (*Reading*) "The New York Democratic Party considers Franklin D. Roosevelt its number one choice for Governor."

ELEANOR Oh, Louie, those items you manage to squeeze into the newspapers are good reading but they're pointless.

HOWE They're good for his morale—and mine. (ELEANOR *still has her mind on the previous scene with* ANNA. LOUIE *senses this*) Your morale looks like it's been hit by a Mack Truck.

ELEANOR I have, on occasion, felt far cheerier, Louie.

HOWE You need a good dinner at Mouquin's— I'll take you out tonight. Clear your head with a bottle of vin rosé and some snails.

ELEANOR Perhaps.

HOWE You're probably scared stiff about that speech you have to read. That's what's wearing you down.

ELEANOR Louie, I'll be no good at it. I can't lecture. I giggle at all the wrong times. I can't control my voice—when I shout I think I'm whispering.

HOWE Eleanor, this work has to be done. You are, for a while, Franklin's eyes, ears—and legs. You must go places he can't go.

ELEANOR I'm certain I'll be awful.

HOWE You are in the hands of Professor Howe—wizard of the spoken word. Speechless mummies given the eloquence of Demosthenes. You don't have to make anything up. Just read it.

ELEANOR I don't like to read a speech.

HOWE Do you think the Gettysburg Address was ad lib?

ELEANOR (*Tired and worn*) I'll try— Leave it at that.

(FDR *suddenly scoots in from the other room*)

FDR (*Seeing* LOUIE) Ah—the pulse taker.

HOWE (*Indicating the papers*) The pulse is good from Maine to California. The nation still endures under Harding. And Teapot Dome is boiling.

FDR (*With finger pointed, as though making a speech*) "Scandals or no scandals—this country will be enduring Republican presidents for a long time unless we rip the barnacles off the Democratic organization and make it a progressive and modern political party." I've just finished writing all that to Cordell Hull.

HOWE Eleanor, that's a good theme for your speech.

FDR My poor retiring Eleanor, being driven into the wilds of the political jungle. Oh, Babs, I invited Marvin and Emmett to dinner—I've got to keep one finger in my lawyer's pie.

ELEANOR We're not very fancy tonight.

FDR My law partners aren't very fussy about their food.

ELEANOR It will be all right.

(*She starts out*)

HOWE Of course it will. I plan to take your wife to Mouquin's tonight for some escargots.

(ELEANOR *is out*)

FDR Eleanor hates rich food. She's too much of a lady to tell you.

HOWE She'll go. It'll do her good to get out of this place for a while. And now, my friend, we have work to do. (*He searches through desk for a pencil*) I have here a list of your various clubs, organizations, federations, fraternities, unions, societies, associations and groups. You and I are going through this list and do a little job of editing.

FDR (*Instantly on guard—irritated*) What exactly have you in mind?

HOWE The doctors say you're doing too much. I'm merely their obedient servant.

FDR (*Changing the subject*) Let me see the list. (*Looks at it*) You have crossed off almost every organization in which I'm genuinely interested.

HOWE Franklin, you have too many interests. You've got to cut down.

FDR I will not discontinue my work in the Boy Scouts. Their aims are damned important.

HOWE What the hell are you working for—scoutmaster?

FDR I'll decide what goes—and what doesn't.

HOWE All right, Franklin, I'll give you the Boy Scouts—but something else has to go. There's a big breeze blowing and we've got to trim sails—the off-year elections. And you've got to keep your hand in.

FDR I won't be able to move around too much for a while.

HOWE But we can write. We can let people know that a man named Roosevelt has opinions, ideas and convictions.

FDR (*Looks at the list*) All right, we can get rid of some of those.

(MISSY *comes in*)

MISSY Mr. Brimmer is here.

HOWE Who's Mr. Brimmer?

FDR It's a deal I'm working on.

HOWE Another?—Oh!—Franklin!

FDR (*To* MISSY) Send him in.

HOWE Missy, who is this Brimmer?

MISSY (*As she exits*) The Boss will tell you.

HOWE Is this another of your imaginative business deals?

FDR Louie, stop heckling me. Just sit quiet.

HOWE I know how you dislike my pacing about.

(HOWE *takes his perch on the couch and remains motionless until indicated.* MISSY *enters with* MR. BRIMMER, *a husky, well-tailored gentleman.* MISSY *exits through the hall door*)

BRIMMER Good day, Mr. Roosevelt. How are you feeling?

FDR Coming along, Mr. Brimmer. Mr. Howe.

(HOWE *waves a greeting*)

BRIMMER Mr. Howe, it's a pleasure.

FDR I've had a long day, Mr. Brimmer— I wonder if—

(*He leaves off.* BRIMMER *understands*)

BRIMMER I have the full picture ready for presentation. Beginning with the estimates on the construction of the four dirigibles as you requested.

HOWE Dirigibles?

FDR Go ahead, Mr. Brimmer.

(MR. BRIMMER *goes ahead. He is a talker and a walker, and his pacing, it is abvious, gets on* FDR'*s nerves, since he is forced to follow* BRIMMER'*s actions. As he begins to talk, a telephone begins to ring in the office offstage*)

BRIMMER The cost of construction, as you will see, will be cheaper if the dirigibles are built in Germany. Airports and masts could be constructed in suitable locations in Chicago and New York for a daily service, at comparatively low cost. Also included, on this sheet, is the amount of helium gas needed—the cost—the construction—items for storage tanks, et cetera, et cetera, et cetera. Also listed, the approximate cost of personnel to run the ships on a daily basis—the airport crew—ticket agencies—and an advertising allotment, based on minimal efforts until the service catches the public fancy.

FDR (*Trying to stop the flow*) It will catch on.

BRIMMER (*Nothing will stop him*) I agree—absolutely—I agree. Charted for you are various hours suggested for best air time in connection with commuter trains, auto traffic and accessibility. Also—ideas for campaigns—all to be studied—digested—assimilated and collated—all to be—

(*The phone in the other room has continued to ring since* BRIMMER *started his long speech. This ringing, combined with* BRIMMER'S *walking has made* FDR *edgy.* HOWE, *who has not moved a muscle till now, gets up to answer the phone*)

FDR (*Exploding*) Louie, why the hell are you always moving around?

HOWE (*Stops, surprised, but knowing in an instant*) I'm nervous.

(*He retreats quietly to the corner. The phone in the next room stops ringing*)

FDR Mr. Brimmer—leave all this here with me. I'll study it in detail—and be in touch with you.

BRIMMER We're prepared to seek underwriting—

FDR We can talk of that later. Thank you, Mr. Brimmer. I'm afraid you'll have to excuse me.

BRIMMER Of course, I understand. I'll leave these estimates. (*To* HOWE) It's been a great pleasure, Mr. Howe.

(*Again the airy acknowledgment from* HOWE)

HOWE Thank you, sir.

MR. BRIMMER And good day to you, Mr. Roosevelt.

FDR Good-bye, Mr. Brimmer. (BRIMMER *is out*) Why the devil didn't someone answer the phone?

HOWE I don't know. I also don't know about dirigibles. What's this scheme?

FDR A damn practical one.

HOWE From New York to Chicago?

FDR For a starter. We can build this into a transcontinental line—eventually nonstop, coast to coast.

HOWE Well—

FDR Don't wet-blanket this, Louie. It could mean a fortune. (HOWE *nods—not a word*) And I'm sorry I yelled. Brimmer was driving me mad. Prowling back and forth—like an awkward tiger.

HOWE With a little helium I'll bet he could get to Chicago.

(FDR *laughs—breaking his irritation and bad spell.* ELEANOR *enters*)

ELEANOR That must have been a good one.

FDR Louie's a monster.

HOWE Madam, your husband is planning to go into the lighter-than-aircraft business—which proves he has a lighter-than-air head.

FDR Caution, my friend, is the refuge of cowards.

ELEANOR And your refuge, Franklin, is bed. You must rest before dinner.

FDR Very well. (*Hesitates*) Today—I'm going upstairs on my own. (*He wheels to the couch*) Out of this room and up the steps on my own. (*To* HOWE) —Without helium. This is something I've been planning for quite a few days.

(*He pulls himself out of the chair and onto the couch*)

ELEANOR (*Anxiously*) Franklin—perhaps it would be wiser if you waited—

FDR No—now is the time. I can crawl, and I'm going to prove it.

HOWE Franklin, it's been a long day.

FDR I'm going to crawl upstairs to bed. (*He gets on the floor*) Stand back, Louie. Bring the chair. Watch me go. (*Sitting on his haunches and using his hands to move his body, he slides backward on the floor and toward the door. As he does,* ELEANOR *and* HOWE *stand frozen.* FDR *continues speaking*) This method of locomotion I shall call the Roosevelt slide: half waltz, half foxtrot. Easy on the feet, placing all the wear and tear on the derrière. (*He is near the door*) Well, Eleanor? Good?

ELEANOR Wonderful, Franklin, wonderful.

FDR See you later.

(*He is out. After a moment,* LOUIE *wheels the chair out of the room, following* FDR. ELEANOR *stands for a moment, then sinks into a chair. She passes a tired hand over her face. She is about to crack, but manages to hold on as the front door is heard to open*)

SARA'S VOICE (*Offstage*) Good day, everybody—

(*Also heard are* FRANKLIN JR.'S *and* JOHNNY'S *voices*)

FRANKLIN JR.'S VOICE Mummy—Mummy—

(ELEANOR *quickly composes herself.* SARA *enters with* FRANKLIN JR. *and* JOHNNY, *who cross over to* ELEANOR)

ELEANOR Hello, boys. Ma*ma.*

SARA I picked them up at school. Saved Mademoiselle a trip. And I wanted to try out their French.

ELEANOR *Les leçons, comment vont elles?*

JOHNNY *Très bien.*

FRANKLIN JR. *Absolument. Très bien.*

JOHNNY Will you read us the end of yesterday's story?

FRANKLIN JR. You promised.

ELEANOR All right. Wash up and come back. I'll keep my promise.

(*The children go—in a hurry*)

SARA Is Franklin in the study?

ELEANOR No, Ma*ma,* he's upstairs. He went up by himself. Crawling.

SARA (*Shocked*) Crawling?

ELEANOR Yes. It's something he's been practicing by himself. He surprised me today by giving me a demonstration.

SARA But that's too much of a strain. He tries too hard—that's bad for him.

ELEANOR Ma*ma*—how can it be bad for him? It makes him independent.

SARA He can't be seen by the children moving around like that—he can't.

ELEANOR You'll have to discuss that with him. I won't. I can't.

SARA Very well, Eleanor. I will speak to him.

ELEANOR Ma*ma,* please allow Franklin the freedom of his own mind in this matter.

SARA He must not be permitted to place such a strain on his body.

ELEANOR Ma*ma,* he's not a child.

SARA Eleanor, perhaps there are times when a son will speak only to his mother.

(JOHNNY *and* FRANKLIN JR. *come bursting back in*)

JOHNNY Come on, Mummy. Sit down, Granny.

SARA No, darlings, I can't. I have to speak to your father. (*She goes.* ELEANOR *wearily moves to a bookcase, chooses the book she was reading, and sits down.* JOHNNY *and* FRANKLIN JR. *sit near her.* ELEANOR *is tired and the children see it—but of course don't take it seriously*)

FRANKLIN JR. Mommy, you look tired.

ELEANOR (*Searching for her place in the book*) I am a little, darling.

JOHNNY Mommy, who is older—you or Granny?

(ELEANOR *looks at* JOHNNY)

FRANKLIN JR. Granny is—you dummy!

ELEANOR (*Beginning to read—trying to fight her emotions*) "And today being Wednesday, the merry old shoemaker knew that he could only work on the blue shoes which were the only ones that were quiet and still on Wednesday. On all the other days the blue shoes would run and play with all the other brightly colored shoes, but on Wednesday they were still and obedient. 'Oh, my,' said the shoemaker, 'what beautiful blue shoes.' And he thought to himself that he would make them even more beautiful. So he took his hammer and nails and sat down—and merrily began to hammer away. . . ."

(Suddenly, unexpectedly and uncontrollably, ELEANOR *begins to cry. She drops the book, turns away from the children and breaks into heartbreaking sobs. The children, stunned, look at her.* MISSY *enters—sees the scene and rushes the children out.* ELEANOR, *left alone, continues to cry. After a few moments,* LOUIE HOWE *appears. It is obvious he has been told, because he enters quietly, expecting to see* ELEANOR. *He closes the door behind him)*

HOWE Eleanor, if I can do anything—

ELEANOR *(Shouting through her tears)* No—nothing—and, Louie, I hate Mouquin's and I hate snails and I'm not going.

HOWE Nobody ever lived who is more entitled to a good cry.

*(*ELEANOR *stops, the well drying. She wipes her eyes—her nose. She straightens her hair)*

ELEANOR I must have terrified the children. *(She gets hold of herself)* I won't ever do that again. Not ever.

(She exits as

The Curtain Falls

SCENE TWO

Scene: We are once again in the New York house living room. In one corner of the room, next to the couch, are a pair of crutches and FDR's *leg braces. It is January, 1923. Friday. Late afternoon.*

At rise: On the floor are ELLIOTT, FRANKLIN JR. *and* FDR. *A wrestling match which has been in progress, accompanied by yells and groans from the two boys, is finally ended when* FDR, *holding* FRANKLIN JR. *with his powerful right hand and* ELLIOTT *with his equally powerful left, swings them both on their backs and holds them there against their will.*

FDR Say uncle!

ELLIOTT (*Still struggling*) Not me!

FDR (*Applying pressure*) Just for that, you young lout—you will now have to say Uncle—Hiram—Joshua—Lafcadio—Turntable.

ELLIOTT Ouch.

(FRANKLIN JR., *assuming* FDR *is occupied with* ELLIOTT, *has made a move to get away*)

FDR Oh, no, you don't.

(*Now* FDR *applies further pressure on* FRANKLIN JR., *without relaxing any on* ELLIOTT)

FRANKLIN JR. Uncle.

FDR Uncle who?

FRANKLIN JR. Uncle—Hiram—Joshua—Lafcadio—

FDR Turntable.

FRANKLIN JR. Turntable!

(FDR *frees* FRANKLIN JR., *who rises, rubbing his muscles*)

ELLIOTT (*Quickly*) I'm outnumbered. Uncle.

FDR Uncle who?

ELLIOTT Uncle Hiram Joshua Lafcadio Turntable.

FDR (*Releases* ELLIOTT, *then sits up on the floor*) Next time I shall improvise a few more names for our fictitious uncle. (*Extends his arms*) Up we go. (*In a manner indicating this is standard procedure,* FRANKLIN JR. *whips over the wheel chair, turns it into correct position, then he and* ELLIOTT *reach out, grab* FDR's *legs*) One—two—three. (*They lift.* FDR, *timing the moves, grabs the chair with his hands, and in a moment he is sitting in his chair, smiling and confident*) You two are getting harder to handle. Soon I'll have to draw out my heavy artillery.

ELLIOTT For a minute we almost had you, Pa.

FDR Delusions of grandeur. (ELLIOTT *and* FDR *laugh*) Boys—today I felt a little more power from my legs. (*Points to his thighs*) Down these heavy frontal muscles—the quadriceps. (*Illustrating on his body*) The bad spots we're still working on are in these thick muscles that run from the hips and buttocks—the gluteus maximus—and then these ham-string muscles on the back of the knees—the gastrocs. Without those I can't get balance or purchase.

FRANKLIN JR. I like the name of those thick muscles.

FDR The gluteus maximus—right there.

FRANKLIN JR. That's it—gluteus maximus.

FDR Once I get them all going at the same time, you'd better start running. (MISSY *enters with the inevitable stack of letters and her notes, together with a framed object*) Enter Missy. Vamoose, sons. Your father is a busy man. I'll give you another lesson tomorrow.

FRANKLIN JR. That's a promise?

FDR That's a promise.

(*They start out*)

ELLIOTT (*To* FRANKLIN JR.) I'll race you upstairs.

(*They dash out*)

(FDR *by now has rolled his chair to his desk. He is already reading and signing letters* MISSY *has placed there for him.* MISSY *hands* FDR *the framed object*)

MISSY This came in by messenger.

FDR (*Examines the object*) A lovely job of printing. (*He looks up at* MISSY) I sometimes regret having told the newspapers one of my favorite poems was "Invictus."

MISSY This is the fourteenth copy you have received.

FDR (*Examining it*) By all odds the most beautiful. I'd like it hung in my bedroom. (*He hands it back to* MISSY, *who places it on the table*) Missy, these letters to the polio victims. They don't sound stuffy, do they?

MISSY No. They're warm and kind.

FDR (*Laughs as he signs the letter*) McAdoo is so excited over the success of the Democrats in the off-year election, he's already started counting the votes for himself in nineteen twenty-four.

MISSY He can taste the nomination.

FDR He's in for a large and bitter disappointment. It's going to be Al Smith.

(*He proceeds with the other letters.* HOWE *and* ELEANOR *come in.* HOWE *is unwrapping himself from a muffler, heavy coat and gloves.* ELEANOR *is dressed warmly, but not heavily*)

ELEANOR We're home.

FDR Welcome back!

HOWE You wouldn't be so damned cheerful if you had to go out in this weather. (*Looks at* ELEANOR) How the hell she stands it, I don't know.

ELEANOR It's lovely and clear outside.

HOWE (*A groan*) Oh, my God. It's freezing. (*He notices the copy of "Invictus" on the table. He picks it up*) "Invictus." Another rendition of that sticky verse. Franklin, the devotion of your admirers is stifling.

(*He puts it back on the table*)

FDR (*To* ELEANOR) How did it go?

(ELEANOR *points to* HOWE, *indicating he has the answer*)

HOWE Your wife has almost rid herself of those ridiculous giggles, and she even manages to make a point now and then with some measure of effectiveness.

FDR (*Interpreting*) You mean—she was good.

HOWE Adequate.

ELEANOR Thank you, teacher.

MISSY Was it a good turnout, Mrs. R?

ELEANOR Excellent. About three hundred women.

HOWE Five hundred. That's the figure I gave the press.

MISSY Five hundred is a lot of people.

ELEANOR So is three hundred. They listened and signed pledges to work. Oh, Franklin, I read your statement on the League of Nations to the Council and it received genuinely warm applause.

FDR Good. Between your speeches, Howe's shenanigans and my statements, we're keeping my head above water.

HOWE (*Standing up*) Speaking of water—I received a letter this morning from one of your associates in the late lamented lobster business.

FDR (*A wince*) A jarring intrusion, as usual.

HOWE He wishes to know whether you have been permanently discouraged by the stubborn refusal of the lobster market to raise its prices.

FDR Losing twenty-six thousand dollars in a lobster business is hardly a joking matter.

HOWE A bit of a pinch—one might say.

FDR To further add to your merriment—this is a letter from the Montracol Oil Company—

(*He hands the letter to* HOWE)

HOWE Oil company—huh?

FDR Good?

HOWE (*As he reads the letter*) Ah—that's very good. You now have two thousands shares—of gas.

ELEANOR What's this one, Franklin?

FDR This has to do with the investment I made in oil. They didn't strike oil—they found gas. And there's no immediate market in gas.

HOWE Think how you could have combined this gas discovery with the dirigibles. (*Starts to the door*) See you for dinner.

(*He exits, coughing and smoking*)

MISSY He'll probably keep coughing and smoking till he's ninety—but sometimes he worries me.

ELEANOR Franklin, if the incense he burns in his room at night gives him some peace from coughing, why don't you let him burn it here? I wouldn't mind.

FDR I would. He'd have the entire place smelling like a bawdy house.

ELEANOR (*Shocked*) Franklin!

FDR Ma*ma* made remarks about it this morning—not quite as indelicate—but pointed. (*To* MISSY) Let's call it a day, Missy. You're going to the country for the week end?

MISSY That's me. Twenty above zero and I'm off for a holiday.

FDR Have fun.

ELEANOR Good night, Missy. I hope it warms up.

MISSY Thank you. Good night, Boss—Mrs. R.

(FDR *waves her a good night as she exits*)

FDR Really went well?

(ELEANOR *nods, then listens*)

ELEANOR The house is quiet. The children—are they all home?

FDR Can't tell the players without a score card, ma'am. (*Counts on his fingers*) Anna is in her room, reading. Johnny is being read to by Mademoiselle. Jimmy ostensibly is still at Groton. Elliott and Franklin have retired to lick their wounds after a wrestling match.

ELEANOR I can't stop you from doing that—but do be careful. Your legs haven't healed completely from that last fall.

FDR They're coming along fine. (*He wheels over to the couch*) All four of them. I spent some time on those today. Soon it will be canes. First I want to handle those crutches without braces—or vice versa.

ELEANOR Of course.

FDR (*Smiles at her*) Of course, you say. As if you mean it. (*He pulls himself onto the couch from the chair*)

ELEANOR I do mean it. It's just that I don't want you to rush and do any damage. You've plenty of time, Franklin.

FDR I've been learning something about time. Being unable to rush things along has given me patience. Patience, I think, gives a better sense of when to try for the brass ring—or when to enjoy the ride without grasping for anything.

ELEANOR Oh, yes, Franklin.

FDR Eleanor, when I first took ill I planned and dreamed about a bright future—half believing, half pretending, like a child on a carousel imagining himself a general in command of armies. But for weeks now something has been changing inside of me. I don't know when it began. What minute or day or hour—but today I was suddenly aware that, despite everything, I feel sure-footed.

ELEANOR "A patient man shall bear for a time and afterward joy shall spring up unto him."

FDR Shall spring up unto us. I sometimes wonder how many of your cousins are still confounded that we married. Do you think they still consider me a feather duster?

ELEANOR (*Smiling*) Darling—(*Then, teasing*) There are undoubtedly some of your family who still believe that you didn't get much of a bargain.

FDR I imagine they're reconciled to the truth that I did better than you did. Actually, I think Ma*ma*'s only objection to you was that your family said *Rusevelt* while we said *Roosevelt*.

ELEANOR Could not a *Rusevelt* by any other name be just as sweet?

FDR (*Laughing*) Not to Ma*ma*. Thinking back, I can hardly blame some of your relatives. I had a lot to learn, but I didn't want anyone to know it. So the truth is I was an awfully mean cuss in those early days.

ELEANOR Never mean. Perhaps inexperienced.

FDR I was snobbish—haughty. I had the Roosevelt name—the Teddy tradition—(*Imitates Teddy's broad smile*)—sauced in with ambition. (*He pats her hand*) I had to learn something about the human heart. (*He smiles at her*) I've been learning.

ELEANOR You have always known a great deal about my heart.

FDR Cousin—wife—dearest.

ELEANOR (*Holding his hands and looking directly at him*) Franklin, when I was an awkward adolescent I felt unloved and unwanted—with you I have always felt needed—wanted—and that's a blessing for which—

(*The door suddenly opens and* ANNA *comes in*)

ANNA Hello, Mother. How are you, Father.

FDR (*Sharply*) Sis, you've developed an irritating habit of barging into rooms without knocking on doors.

ANNA (*Instantly hurt*) I wanted to put these books back.

FDR Then do it, Sis. (ANNA *is shocked by the harsh greeting and command. She is on the verge of tears. Starting to put the books away, she loses control of them and they clatter to the floor*) That's a stupid, clumsy way to do it.

(ANNA *breaks into tears and runs out of the room.* ELEANOR *and* FDR *exchange a look*)

ELEANOR Rather a sharp attack for a mild offense.

FDR I'll make it up to her later.

ELEANOR I'd best talk to her before she runs to Granny.

(*She picks up the books* ANNA *dropped*)

FDR Oh—Ma*ma* is coming for dinner.

ELEANOR Oh—

FDR I do hope she and Louie don't snap at each other. Last time they went as far as the dessert before sharp words.

ELEANOR That's because at the moment Ma*ma* has one objective—Louie, another.

FDR I intend to talk to Ma*ma* about it.

ELEANOR Usually your talks with Ma*ma* last for fifteen minutes—then they become quarrels.

FDR I'll time it. Make sure it's a talk.

(HOWE *enters the room*)

HOWE Change of plans. I spoke to Grace. She's been wondering if I've gotten any uglier. Also, Hartley looked at the postman this morning and wondered if that was Daddy. So I'm going home for dinner. (*He is picking up his muffler, overshoes and hat from where he had left them. He wraps himself up in his clothes, coughing*) Oh, I thought I should report. Anna is seated in the upper hallway, looking as though she has been axed and maced.

ELEANOR I'll try to alleviate the pain. Good night, Louie.

HOWE Good night.

(ELEANOR *leaves.* FDR *looks at* HOWE, *who is huddled in his coat and muffler*)

FDR Can you breathe through all that?

HOWE You know me. If I'm on my feet I assume I'm breathing.

FDR Louie, I'm being reflective.

HOWE Well, that's probably because you're heading for another birthday.

FDR Having made this one, everything after is velvet. (*A moment*) Part of my reflections had to do with you.

HOWE Ah—I'm fired?

FDR (*He takes* HOWE's *hand*) My good friend, as much as you loathe a sentimental moment, thank you for everything.

(HOWE *heads toward the door but pauses at the table on which rests the framed copy of "Invictus." He hesitates, picks up the framed poem, eyes it critically, and looks at* FDR, *who has been watching him all through this.* HOWE *loosens his muffler, takes a mock heroic pose, and then, in a Dutch accent, begins to recite, doing a burlesque rendition*)

HOWE Out of der night that covers me,
Black as der Pit from pole to pole,
I tank whatever Gods may be
For mine unconquerable soul.

In der vell clutch of circumstance
I haf not vinced nor cried aloud.
Under der bludgeonings of chance
Mine head is ploody but unbowed.

(Slowly, during the next two verses, he drops the accent and begins to recite clearly and beautifully—and we see now that what he has been doing is giving a tribute to FDR*)*

Beyond this place of wrath and tears
Looms but the Horror of the shade,
And yet the menace of the years
Finds, and shall find, me unafraid.

It matters not how strait the gate,
How charged with punishments the scroll,
I am the master of my fate:
I am the captain of my soul.

(As he has finished, he has spoken slowly, movingly. FDR *looks at him.* HOWE, *when he has finished, looks at* FDR. *There is a pause)*

'Night.

(He walks out. ANNA *appears at the doorway, followed by* ELEANOR. ANNA *knocks gently on the door.* FDR *looks up, smiles at her, and then he knocks on the desk in answer)*

ANNA *(Crossing over)* Father.

FDR Hello, Sis. I'm an old grouch.

(They embrace)

ANNA Father, I've been selfish.

FDR Now, Sis—no confessionals.

ANNA I have been. (FDR *directs that she bring his wheel chair to him. She does so*) I've been mooning around the house like a child—I felt everybody was keeping me out of rooms. I didn't really understand what you've been going through.

(FDR *pulls himself into the wheel chair*)

ELEANOR I've been to blame for some of that. We should have talked before.

ANNA That's all I ask, Mother. Please talk. Everyone is so occupied—

ELEANOR We'll all try to find more time.

ANNA (*Turning to* FDR) And about my room, Father. I actually prefer it upstairs. (*She smiles*) It's quieter.

FDR Anna dear, most of our blessings come in heavy disguises. (*He moves his chair towards her*) Which, of course, reminds me of a story. 'Way back in the hills of Upstate New York, where a lot of poor tenant farmers live, there was a wise old man whom everybody came to with their troubles. One day a woman came to him with a sad story. She and her husband and four children lived in a one-room cabin and she said it was simply unbearable. The old man asked her if she had any chickens on the farm. When she said she had, he advised her to put the chickens in her house. The next day she came back and said that things were even worse—much worse. Then the old man asked if she owned any cows, and when she said she had two of them, he said: "Put those cows in your house." She did and the next day she came back and said the place was getting to be a horror. So the old man said to her: "You got a horse?" She said she did. "Put the horse into your house." The woman did that, too, and the following day said it was just too much—it was awful. Then the old man said to her, "Well, my dear, now take the horse and those cows and those chickens and get them all out of there—and then come back and tell me how things are." And the next day the woman came back and said: "Thank you, oh, thank you so much. You can't imagine how comfortable we all are at last."

ANNA (*With a warm smile*) Thank you, Father, for not putting the chickens in my room.

FDR (*With a smile*) Sis, in the last two minutes, you've grown ten years wiser.

SARA'S VOICE (*Offstage*) Good evening, everyone—good evening.

ELEANOR We're in here.

SARA'S VOICE (*Offstage*) Franklin, too?

FDR Yes, ma'am. Present.

(SARA *enters, loosening her coat and removing her gloves*)

SARA There you are. Anna, you look lovely. (ANNA *curtsies.* SARA *crosses to* FDR *and kisses him*) It's bitterly cold. Like a frosty night at sea. (*A long look at* FDR) Franklin, you look peaked.

FDR I feel fine.

SARA You're doing too much. I can tell.

FDR (*As a reassuring sign to* ELEANOR, *but talking to* SARA) I won't quarrel with you. If you say I looked peaked—I look peaked.

SARA (*Taking off her things*) Anna, be a darling. (*Hands her gloves and coat and hat and muff to* ANNA) *Tu est très gentille, ma petite.*

ANNA (*Deliberately avoiding any French*) Thank you, Granny.

ELEANOR A cup of tea, Ma*ma?*

SARA I'd love some. (*To* ANNA, *as* ELEANOR *exits*) How are all my darlings?

ANNA (*With a smile*) The boys are as dreadful as ever. And so am I.

SARA Were you outdoors today?

ANNA For a while.

SARA You have to remember to bundle up warm. Overshoes, gloves and something soft and wooly around your neck.

ANNA I know.

SARA Nurse should be very careful with the young ones in weather like this.

ANNA (*After a deep breath*) I heard Mother telling Nurse that this morning.

(*This is possibly the first time* ANNA *has taken this unspoken attitude toward Granny. There is a brief recognition of this by* SARA *and* FDR. *A pause*)

SARA Very sensible.

(ANNA *exits with Granny's things.* ELEANOR *comes in with a tray of tea*)

ELEANOR Cream, Ma*ma?*

SARA Please.

(ELEANOR *pours the tea.* ANNA *returns and stands by*)

ELEANOR Franklin?

FDR No cream—no lemon—four sugars.

SARA Cream is good for you, Franklin.

FDR I don't like cream in my tea.
(ANNA *hands Granny her tea, then hands* FDR *his*)

SARA Thank you, dear.

FDR Sis.
(ELEANOR *hands* ANNA *a cup*)

ANNA Mother, may I have mine upstairs? I want to finish something I've been reading.

ELEANOR Of course.

ANNA Excuse me, Granny, Father—
(*She goes out*)

SARA Anna looks well.

FDR But I look peaked.

SARA Franklin—stop being a tease.

ELEANOR (*Not staying for tea*) I'm afraid I'll have to be excused. I've got to check on the children. We're all eating together tonight and later we're going to read some Shakespeare.

SARA I hope one of the comedies. So much of Shakespeare is too lurid for children.

FDR (*The crier*) Tonight—*As You Like It.*

SARA Lovely.

ELEANOR Excuse me, please.

SARA Of course, dear. (ELEANOR *leaves.* SARA *sips her tea, thinking of the opening gambit. She finds one*) Oh, Franklin, I'm getting some men at Hyde Park to determine how we can electrify the lift. It is, after all, only a large-size dumbwaiter and I—

FDR (*Quickly*) No! (*Perhaps he's been too sharp*) I mean, please don't. The exercise of pulling those ropes is helpful to me. I need it for my arms and shoulders. So, if you're thinking of me—please don't change the dumbwaiter.

SARA I feel you're doing too much, physically.

FDR I wish I could do more. Ma*ma*—it's only my legs that are temporarily bothered. The rest of me is as healthy as ever.

SARA I know that. I know that. I talk to the doctors. They tell me. But sometimes I think that Eleanor, certainly only with motives of deep love, and that ugly little man, push you too rapidly.

FDR I don't think so. Dr. Draper doesn't think so. And please, Ma*ma,* don't refer to Louie Howe any longer with that unpleasant phrase. I've endured it too long as it is.

SARA (*Walking about, genuinely disturbed*) Franklin, your tone of voice is very disturbing to me.

FDR Ma*ma,* if possible, I should like to have a quiet talk with you. I should like not to quarrel. Now, Ma*ma,* I know how upset you've been. This a real wrench for you. But I'm going to get over this—and—if I don't—a big *if*—I shall have to become accustomed to braces and canes and wheel chairs. And so will you.

SARA Oh, Franklin—

FDR Please, let me finish. Louie Howe—(SARA *makes an involuntary grimace*) Ma*ma,* stop that. Louie Howe told me, while I was in the hospital after Campobello, that I had one of two choices. I could lie on my back, be a country squire and write books—*or*—get up and become President of the United States. *Now*—I believe Louie's dreams are far too bright—but I've no intention of retiring to Hyde Park and rusticating.

SARA (*Quietly*) Franklin, when you were a little boy, your dear father took you for a visit to the White House to see President Cleveland.

FDR (*Fidgets*) Ma*ma,* I know.

SARA (*Firmly*) Let me finish. And President Cleveland said, "I make a strange wish for you. It is that you may never be President of the United States."

FDR Well, he was playing the odds in wishing that.

SARA Your Cousin Teddy died because of ambitious people around him. Died because he didn't know when to stop—didn't know that you can't make it the same world for all people.

FDR Maybe we can't. But it seems to me that every human has an obligation in his own way to make some little stab at trying.

SARA It's not such a bad world, Franklin—not at all.

FDR I have no personal complaints. I'm lucky. I had rich parents.

SARA Don't be self-conscious about that, Franklin. Advantages of birth should be worn like clothes, with grace and comfort.

FDR (*A familiar tale—and he knows it*) Yes—yes. *Noblesse oblige*. The poor will always be with us. We went through that when I sold the mining stock.

SARA On reflection—you must admit that was a childish gesture.

FDR (*The heat is on*) I would not hang onto stock bringing me an income over the tortured bodies of miners who lived as though they were in the middle ages. These are different times. The attitude of *noblesse oblige* is archaic.

SARA Franklin!

FDR It's another name for indifference.

SARA How dare you! You are talking to your mother. Even if I were to agree with your romantic political ideas, it would be absurd for you to consider running for public office. The traveling and the speeches would be an enormous strain for you.

FDR At the moment I'm not running for anything—and I won't until I can get around and stand up on my two feet—but that doesn't mean I have to go into hiding.

SARA (*Icily*) I'm not asking you to do that. I'm asking you to be sensible—to take up a permanent residence in Hyde Park where you could be comfortable—where you could use the time for resting and regain your strength.

FDR I love Hyde Park. But I want to use it—not let it bury me.

SARA That's a terrible thing to say.

FDR You know what I mean.

SARA No, Franklin, I do not know what you mean. I only know that your stubbornness is not only your strength but your weakness. And you needn't—

FDR (*Getting angry*) I needn't do a damn thing! I am not going to let myself go down a drain. A bad beating either breaks the stick or the student— Well, I'm not broken. I'm not settling for the life of an ailing invalid. And I will no longer abide implications, innuendos or insinuations that I do so.

SARA I don't want you getting angry. It's not good for you.

FDR (*Heatedly*) It's damn good. For me.

SARA Franklin, I wonder if you truly know what is good for you. You come by your Dutch stubbornness by birth. And, Franklin, some of that Dutch stubbornness is mine—from long association. (*She now becomes firm and dominant*) Franklin, many many years ago, when I was a little girl, I sailed to China with my father on a clipper ship. As we rounded Cape Horn, we headed into a fearful storm. My father, eager and headstrong, urged the Captain to head into the sea—to fight through the storm. But fortunately the Captain of the ship was a better sailor than my father. He wanted to save his ship. He trimmed sails, gave orders to "heave to," rode out the storm safely, and then, when the heavy weather was gone, we were able to sail ahead and nothing was lost—nothing. Be wise, Franklin—ride out the storm. (*A pause.* SARA, *emotionally wrought-up by now, strikes hotter*) Son, let me ask you—what do you believe I want for you—obscurity? Invalidism? Do you believe that this is my ambition for you? Having been a mother for over forty years, do you think this is what I want? Any dream you ever had or could have, I have. All pain you have felt, I have felt. (*By now she is sharp and hard*) I don't want to see you hurt.

FDR That's enough. There'll be no more talking—no more. (SARA *goes to the side of the room. She is moved and hurt, but genuinely trying to cover her emotions.* FDR *has discarded his pipe and is trying to cover what he feels. At this moment,* ELEANOR *enters. She sees at a glance that there is tension in the room.* SARA *turns her back a moment, then faces* ELEANOR, *contained but cold*)

SARA Eleanor, I cannot have dinner with you tonight.

ELEANOR Ma*ma*—you may have quarreled with Franklin—but not with the rest of the family. (SARA *is mum*) Please?

SARA (*Reluctantly*) Very well—I'll join you. Excuse me. (ELEANOR *nods.* SARA *looks at* FDR. *He by now is depressed rather than angry.* SARA *leaves.* ELEANOR *watches* FDR, *who sits glumly in his chair for a moment, then whirls around to her*)

ELEANOR Franklin, anything needed?

FDR Nothing.

(ELEANOR *hesitates a moment, then exits.* FDR *sits for a moment. He is low and dispirited. Suddenly he looks up and toward the crutches. He is in his mind challenging his mother and what she has implied. He decides to prove something to himself and to her. He quickly rolls his chair to the crutches. He places them on his knees and then moves to a clearer section of the room. He puts up one crutch, and then the other, attempting to rise off the chair by himself and onto the crutches. He is confident and determined. He is half out of the chair when the crutch slips away from him and he crumples to the floor. He lies there a moment, a look of sickening defeat and humiliation and pain on his face. He rubs his leg. Then, alarmed that perhaps he has been heard, he attempts to get back into his chair. This is not an easy task, but slowly, carefully and painfully, he manages—again almost meeting disaster, but finally overcoming his obstacles, he makes the security and safety of his chair. He pauses, exhausted and in pain. Then he reaches for his crutches, rolls the chair to each crutch successively, and finally by stretching and bending, gets them into his hands and over his knees. He sits now, his head bent forward, a portrait of a man who has lost a battle that seemed so very important. Slowly he leans back, his face now hard and grim, but determined. Then, stubbornly, he places the crutches before him and prepares to try again to rise from the chair. He begins his efforts, but we do not know if he succeeds or not, as*

The Curtain Falls

ACT THREE

ACT THREE

Scene One

Scene: It is May, 1924. We are again in the New York house. Spring flowers are in vases. It is a sunny spring day.

At rise: Seated in the room is MR. LASSITER. *He is a middle-aged man. He is well dressed and carries an air of authority. He looks at his watch, steals a look at the door leading into the room, and then returns his gaze to the outdoors.*

The door opens and FDR, *wheeling his chair, enters the room. Behind him is* HOWE.

FDR How do you do, Mr. Lassiter. Mr. Howe—

LASSITER Mr. Roosevelt.

FDR I regret I had to keep you waiting, because I've been looking forward to this meeting.

LASSITER Mr. Roosevelt, I know that your time is terribly occupied. But what I have to talk to you about is of great importance.

FDR (*With a smile*) I recognized the note of urgency in your telegrams.

(*Wheels his chair near the table.* HOWE *takes his familiar perch on the sofa and* FDR *motions to* LASSITER *to sit down*)

LASSITER You of course know something of the organization I represent.

FDR I do indeed.

LASSITER We have in recent months enlarged the scope of our work and we hope very shortly to have a national pattern of activity. (FDR *nods*) Your name, Mr. Roosevelt, has stood for something important among the rank and file of our membership.

FDR Please thank the rank and file.

LASSITER I will come directly to the point. Your chairmanship of Governor Smith's campaign for the Presidential nomination has caused much apprehension among many—many of our members.

FDR (*Knowing instantly what the issues are going to be*) That's curious, Mr. Lassiter. What causes this apprehension?

LASSITER Because of our opposition to Governor Smith, we view with alarm your association with and your sponsorship of his cause.

FDR I for one am very flattered at my association with Governor Smith. What is there about him that induces this opposition from your membership, Mr. Lassiter?

LASSITER (*Confidentially*) Mr. Roosevelt, I don't think it necessary for me to dot the i's and cross the t's.

FDR I love to dot the i's and cross the t's.

LASSITER You must certainly be aware of the fears that many Americans have, when they contemplate the election of a Catholic to the Presidency of the United States. The domination of the church over its members is well known. And Governor Smith is a devout Catholic.

HOWE Would he be more acceptable if he were a renegade Catholic?

FDR (*Chidingly, to* HOWE) Louie— (*Then, after a moment's thought*) It occurs to me, Mr. Lassiter, that your members might be satisfied with a personal statement from me that would enlighten them on my views in this matter.

LASSITER (*Hopefully*) I am certain that a statement of the proper kind from you, Mr. Roosevelt, will be of some service.

FDR I have something in mind. (*Wheels his chair to the office door*) Missy—Missy—(*Rolls his chair back.* MISSY *enters*) Would you be good enough to type up a statement. (*Looks at* LASSITER) How many copies would you like, sir?

LASSITER Oh, one or two would be sufficient, Mr. Roosevelt. We would print it and circulate it for the best effect.

FDR And I will see that it gets proper circulation in other quarters. (*He wheels his chair so that he faces* MISSY *more directly. He culls his thoughts and dictates. In his dictation, his voice becomes sharp, and his manner is the manner so associated with him in later years*) "I am not worried that the Roosevelt name will be tarnished by any association with Governor Smith. If a Catholic who has the ability, broadness of view and fine record that entitled him to be considered Presidential timber, cannot be nominated or elected President because of his religion, then we might just as well be consistent and say he cannot be Governor or Congressman or Mayor or hold any other public office or be called upon to serve in the Army or Navy in defense of his country in war." (*He twists his chair around and looks directly at* LASSITER, *who by now is furious*) Is that what you had in mind, Mr. Lassiter?

LASSITER Good day, Mr. Roosevelt.
(*He stalks out of the room*)

FDR Good day.

HOWE I wonder if there is any way of getting the tone of voice you used, in print.

MISSY Unfortunately there are a lot of people who feel exactly like Mr. Lassiter.

FDR The real issue remains. Is Governor Smith best equipped to be the nominee for the Democratic Party and, ultimately, President of the United States? I think he is.

HOWE In this Year of Our Lord, Nineteen Twenty-four, even if Al Smith were Protestant and "Dry," he couldn't be elected President on the Democratic ticket. If he's the right man, he's running at the wrong time.

MISSY (*Referring to her watch*) Right or wrong, the Governor is about twenty minutes late.

HOWE The Convention isn't till June. We can wait.

FDR (*Glancing at some papers on his desk*) Missy, would you send a note to the Golf Club along with a check for the dues. "I should like my membership changed from active to non-resident." (*There is a pause*) "I can't possibly play golf myself for a year or two." The usual thank you ever and very truly.

MISSY Yes, sir.

FDR (*Taking a brief look at some other papers*) I haven't anything else, Missy. Type up that statement as soon as you can.

MISSY (*Nods and turns to* HOWE *as she starts to exit*) Have anything, Louie?

HOWE Nothing for paper, Missy—just a pocketful of second thoughts.

(FDR *turns to* HOWE *as* MISSY *goes out*)

FDR Second thoughts, Louie? What's worrying you?

HOWE First, breathing. (*He wheezes air into his lungs*) I've been wondering what Al wants to talk to you about this afternoon.

FDR I would suppose it's some genial campaign chatter.

HOWE I think it's something special.

FDR What do your psychic rumblings indicate?

HOWE I haven't yet spelled out all the words on my invisible ouija board.

FDR (*Lightly*) Do you think he regrets his appointment of me as his chairman?

HOWE (*Shaking his head*) He still needs Upstate New York. You're Protestant—Dry—rural. You're the logical cowcatcher. I've been thinking about Burke Cockran.

FDR Why Burke Cockran?

HOWE Ever since Burke died, Smith has been searching for a replacement. He's been trying out speakers to place him in nomination.

FDR If he's finally gotten around to me it must be a reluctant choice.

HOWE Why so?

FDR Oh, Louie, you know that Al has always had a patronizing attitude towards me. (*Imitating* SMITH) "Listen, kid, let me teach you the facts of life in the big city."

HOWE He's one breed of animal. You're another. He made it without a rich family, and he's as good as you are any day.

(FDR *begins to wander about the room in his chair.* HOWE *watches him. A moment*)

FDR It would be odd for a chairman also to nominate. A precedent.

HOWE Would you be up to it?

FDR (*Who has moved from the desk, stops a moment and considers this*) I sometimes wonder if I could stand the gaff of active work. Maybe the aspirations and dreams for public service would disappear in the hard light of practical politics.

HOWE I'm no idle dreamer, Franklin. Working with you is an act of faith. I believe God has an eye on your future.

FDR (*Sharply*) God has an infinite variety of tasks, and I don't believe He's available as a campaign manager.

HOWE Franklin, the problem is this: How to stop a lot of talk from people who say Roosevelt's a nice fellow who once had a fine chance—but isn't it too bad. You might be able to carry the speech off wonderfully and put the party on notice that you're ready for active service. But you could fail and be headed for the political boneyard.

FDR That's a clean picture of the situation.

HOWE Well—

FDR Well, first let's see if Smith begins sizing me up as his nominator.

HOWE And if he does?

FDR Then, Louie, *mein* boy, I'll start sizing him up as my nominee.

(*The door opens and* ELEANOR *enters. She is dressed in afternoon clothes. Her manner is surer and more defined*)

FDR Who's going with you, Eleanor?

ELEANOR I don't need an entourage. I walk in—say my few words—shake a hundred hands, and go on to the next stop.

HOWE (*To* FDR) Why don't you get Eleanor's opinion on what we've been talking about?

FDR Louie has a hunch—and I'm inclined to think he's right—that Al Smith is coming here today to ask me to place him in nomination.

ELEANOR Well, I have heard that he's been shopping around for a speaker.

HOWE (*To* FDR *as he points at* ELEANOR) She hears everything.

FDR (*To* ELEANOR) Well, what do you think?

ELEANOR I think that's a decision that only you can make.

FDR *That's* taking a well-defined position.

ELEANOR I know you'd make a wonderful speech. Whether you're ready to do it is a matter only you can decide.

HOWE What about the risks or advantages politically?

ELEANOR I'm no politician. I have the naïve point of view that in public service one should pursue principles without calculating the consequences.

(FDR *looks at* HOWE *archly*)

HOWE She's right. She's no politician.

(ELEANOR *crosses to* FDR)

ELEANOR Only one point to consider physically. You'd have to stand for almost three-quarters of an hour.

FDR (*Nods*) I would have to go into training for that.

(ELEANOR *crosses to* FDR *and gives him a kiss on the cheek*)

FDR Ummm—I like that cologne.

(ELEANOR *starts out as* MISSY *enters*)

MISSY They're ready, Mr. R.

FDR Oh, Eleanor, take a copy of that, will you. If you find a place to use it this afternoon, rattle it in.

HOWE Hail and farewell!

ELEANOR (*As she exits*) Good-bye.

FDR I think Eleanor is beginning to enjoy this political prowling.

HOWE What's more, she's getting damned good at it. (*The doorbell rings and* HOWE *looks at his watch*) It's late enough. That could be the Governor.

(*We hear sounds from the hallway*)

ELEANOR'S VOICE (*Offstage*) Good afternoon, Governor Smith.

(MISSY *has started out*)

SMITH'S VOICE Hello, Eleanor. And hello, Missy.

MISSY'S VOICE Good afternoon, Governor.

SMITH'S VOICE Why, I've never had a reception from a brace of such beautiful girls. Eleanor, I hear you're getting to be quite a speaker. Glad you're on my side.

ELEANOR'S VOICE The fact that I am makes my speeches sound better.

(FDR *and* HOWE *exchange a look*)

SMITH'S VOICE Hope to see you soon. 'Bye.

MISSY'S VOICE Mr. Roosevelt's in the library, Governor.

(*We hear the sound of the door closing, and in a moment* AL SMITH *enters. He is in his prime—saucy, smart and healthy*)

SMITH Hello, Frank. How're you feeling? Hello, Louie.

FDR Hello, Al.

HOWE Hello, Governor. You're looking fit.

SMITH (*Shakes hands with* FDR) That hand of yours is getting like a vise.

MISSY (*Entering*) Some cold refreshment?

SMITH Why, Missy—there's a law in this country against strong refreshment. An obnoxious law, but nevertheless a law.

MISSY I know. Scotch or rye?

SMITH Scotch, thanks. And don't kill it with soda. (MISSY *exits to mix the drinks*) Frank, I met Eleanor on the way in. She's doing a fine job.

FDR She's been taking her lessons from Professor Howe.

SMITH Louie, you ought to open up a school.

HOWE Any school in practical politics, Governor, would have to have you as the dean.

SMITH Say—I didn't know you could hand out the blarney. (*Turns to* FDR) Frank, I hear you've broken up your law firm with Emmett and Marvin. What's the matter? The work a little too rugged for you?

FDR (*With a smile*) As a matter of fact, Al, it wasn't rugged enough. I did withdraw on the friendliest basis. But their type of work—estates, wills, et cetera—frankly, it bored me to death.

SMITH Certainly keeps you freer to do what you want.

(MISSY *re-enters with the drinks*)

MISSY Your Scotch, Governor. Still alive, I hope.

SMITH (*Trying his drink*) Perfect. Thanks, Missy.

MISSY Yours, Mr. R.

FDR Missy.

MISSY And I brought you a soft drink, Louie.

HOWE Reluctantly—thanks.

MISSY (*As she leaves*) If you need fresh ones, a call will bring you our instant courteous service, available at all hours.

(*She goes out*)

SMITH That girl's a jewel, Frank.

FDR That she is.

(*They sip their drinks*)

SMITH They tell me there's a lot of McAdoo money around town.

HOWE I wish I had some money to bet. Bill isn't going to make it.

SMITH He's coming into town a lot stronger than I thought. You know, Frank, we're putting on a big show here in New York and we can make it look like Smith all through the city, but McAdoo and his organization are coming to this convention with a half-Nelson on all the rules and program machinery. We can get strangled inside Madison Square Garden.

FDR We won't get strangled. Though it's going to be a mighty tough wrestling match.

SMITH I'd like to win this nomination, but there's a good chance it might be a stalemate. (*Takes another sip of his drink*) I was going over the delegate strength with Belle Moscowitz and Joe Proskauer yesterday. (*He looks at* FDR) How do you size it up, Frank?

FDR I don't think you can make it on the first ballot, Al.

SMITH (*With a nod*) That's the way we figured it.

FDR But neither can McAdoo.

SMITH I'll tell you one thing, Frank. If it isn't going to be me, it'll never be McAdoo. I'll fight him with my last breath. Any man who can take the support of an organization like the Ku Klux Klan—he's not my kind of man.

FDR Oh, a letter reached me and I want you to hear part of it. (*He wheels over to his desk*)

SMITH You handle that chair like a scooter.

FDR Practice makes—(*Imitating* SMITH)—poifect, Al. (*Digs into the pile of mail*) It's from Babe Ruth. I asked him to chairman a committee for you.

SMITH The Babe.

FDR (*Picking up the letter*) "No poor boy can go any too high in this world to suit me. You know we ball players travel the country a good deal and I hear lots of fellows talking about Al Smith and his chances to be President and I'm telling you that most everybody I talk to is with him."

(*He puts the letter down*)

SMITH (*With a chuckle*) How many ball players are there?

FDR I hope he's as good a prophet as he is a slugger.

SMITH I sure miss Burke Cockran during these days. He had a great instinct in these subtle matters of conventions, nominations and elections. Sort of spooky. I sure miss him. For many reasons.

FDR (*The first probe*) You certainly would have wanted him to nominate you. There was no one better.

SMITH That's a fact. No one better.

FDR He had a magnificent voice and knew how to use it.

SMITH It wasn't just the way he talked, Frank. He had a knack of saying just the right thing.

FDR (*Nodding*) That he did.

SMITH For days now I've been trying to think what Burke would have wanted to say in a nominating speech.

FDR It seems to me he'd have argued for you as a progressive. He certainly would have been aware of the issues—the Klan—the Volstead Act—and the latent issue of your faith. He might have been willing to point out that the obligation above any one candidate was to keep the party together.

SMITH I'm all for party unity, but I don't intend to temporize on the issue of the Klan. And Burke wouldn't have, either.

FDR I agree that it ought to be burned out once and for all. But if we can't get through a resolution condemning the Klan, we still mustn't break up the party.

SMITH Frank, I remember all my early lessons. One of them was that the first objective of a politician is to be elected. Then he can fight for causes. But in the case of the Klan, I'm willing to forget an early lesson.

FDR (*Nods*) There's another issue, Al. Even more important than the Klan. That's the issue of world politics and America's place in it. Burke would have talked of that, perhaps.

SMITH Frank, if you're talking about the League of Nations, that's a dead dodo.

FDR I think if the Democratic Party is going to stand, it has to stand for something big and noble.

SMITH I suppose there's nothing wrong with mankind having a vision of a world organization. But it's only a vision.

FDR Newton Baker wants to submit a resolution to support the League of Nations at the Convention.

SMITH It hasn't got a chance.

FDR Perhaps not. But I think you ought to support it. Woodrow Wilson's in his grave only three months, and I don't think we ought to let his convictions about the League be buried with him.

SMITH (*Grudgingly*) It's all right with me.

HOWE I'll speak to the Program Committee and have Baker put it on the schedule.

SMITH Frank, got any other notions about what Burke Cockran would have to say?

FDR (*With a smile*) Finally, I think he'd make up his own speech, a large part of which would have to do with the fine record of the man he'd be nominating.

SMITH (*Returning the smile*) I suppose a few kind words about me would be in order. Frank, Burke had a theory that no nominating speech ought to run more than thirty to forty minutes.

FDR You can read the Bill of Rights in that time.

SMITH That's a long time for any man to be on his feet.

FDR You certainly can't make an effective speech sitting down.

SMITH You can be sure of that.

FDR After all the months I've spent in this chair, I've come to love the time I spend each day standing on my crutches.

SMITH Uh-huh.

(*There is a pause.* SMITH *looks at his glass, which is empty*)

HOWE Fresh one, Governor?

SMITH No thanks. (*Puts his glass down*) Frank, I'd like you to put me in nomination.

FDR That's a surprise.

(*He looks at* LOUIE)

HOWE Caught me flat-footed.

SMITH Will you do it, Frank?

FDR Certainly.

SMITH I'll want to have a look at what you're going to say, and Joe Proskauer may have an idea or two. He's a good phrase-maker.

FDR I won't mind the addition of a few phrases. But Al, what I say will have to be what I want to say.

SMITH Yes, Frank, you have made that quite clear. (*Looks at his vest-pocket watch*) Say, time runs fast. (*With a wry smile*) I've got some other people I've kept waiting. (*Gets to his feet*) I'm glad you're going to do this, Frank. I appreciate it and won't forget it.

FDR Thank you, Al. I consider it a singular privilege and honor. I'll try to make your choice a good one.

SMITH I'm satisfied you will. Take care, kid.

FDR So long, Al.

SMITH See you, Louie. Say good-bye to Missy.

HOWE I'll take you to the door.

(SMITH *starts to the door, then stops, turns*)

SMITH Frank, did you have an idea I was going to ask you?

FDR A vagrant thought. Why?

SMITH It just occurred to me you were both too surprised to be surprised.

(*He waves his hand and leaves.* HOWE *follows him out.* FDR *scoots to the office door*)

FDR Missy—Missy—(*He rolls back into the room. The front door is heard opening, then closing.* MISSY *enters, just a moment before* HOWE) I'm going to nominate Governor Smith.

MISSY Bravo!

FDR I like him. He's sharp as a blade.

HOWE (*As he enters, it is obvious he is pleased and excited*) I feel like an agent who just had an act booked into the Palace. You have the ball, Franklin. (*Looks at* MISSY) Make him do good, Missy.

MISSY You know me. I write all of Irving Berlin's music and Franklin Roosevelt's speeches.

HOWE Smith will make the announcement tomorrow that you're going to nominate. I'll follow up by flooding him with congratulations.

FDR Louie, ease up. (*He looks at* MISSY) Missy—we have to get a blueprint of that platform at the Garden. I want to know just how far it is from where I'll be sitting to that lectern.

HOWE About ten steps, I'd say, not more.

FDR (*Thinking*) Ten steps. I can do that. I'll take Jimmy with me—he's the biggest. (*Rolls his chair and seems to be measuring*) Ten steps—about twenty feet?

HOWE About.

FDR I'll work on that. We have got to get the exact measurement.

HOWE Work hard, Franklin. (*A pause*) They are liable to be the ten biggest steps you ever took in your life.

(FDR *looks up at* HOWE *questioningly.* MISSY *eyes them both*)

FDR (*Eager to break the solemn mood*) Perhaps—or, to be clinical—I may fall smack on my gluteus maximus.

The Curtain Falls

Scene Two

Scene: We are in a small room of Madison Square Garden. We are aware of the roaring sound of the Convention hall, which is swarming with delegates. The sound is constant and present in the room, but not loud enough to distract us. It is June 26, 1924, about 11:30 P.M.

At rise: In the room is FDR, *seated in a more conventional wheel chair than the ones he has used in his home. He is bronzed and beaming with vitality.* JAMES, *the eldest son, stands near the back wall, on which his father's crutches lean.* ELEANOR *is seated to the left of* FDR, *knitting.* HOWE *is standing by.* MISSY *is seated to the right of* FDR. *A uniformed* POLICEMAN *is on duty, guarding the door. A screen is in one corner of the room, large enough to cover* FDR *and his wheel chair.* FDR's *braces are on the desk. A roar goes up outside.* HOWE *looks at his watch.*

HOWE That, very likely, is the finish of Miss Kennedy's address to the brethren.

ELEANOR Now what?

HOWE Now Bill Sweet, to second the nomination of McAdoo —then the roll call—and if Connecticut remembers its cue, it yields to New York—and—

(*He points to* FDR)

FDR Then they get one half-hour of little ol' me.

(DALY, *a young man, dashes in. He is frantic*)

DALY Mr. Roosevelt, I've checked everything again and again —and everything should be all right.

FDR I'm certain it will be, Daly.

DALY You're feeling okay?

FDR (*Nodding*) Fine.

DALY Is there anything I can do for you, sir?

FDR No, thank you.

HOWE (*Noticing* DALY'S *tension*) Say, Daly—

DALY Yes—

HOWE I'd like to make sure that everything is on schedule. Take a look—size up the crowd—get some impressions and then report back. Will you do that?

DALY Of course.

HOWE Thanks. Thanks very much.

(HOWE *motions to* MISSY *to open the door. She does, as* DALY *approaches it. We see the* POLICEMAN *and hear the crowd, louder now.* DALY *goes out, and the door closes*)

FDR Thanks, Louie.

HOWE I wasn't thinking about you. He was driving me crazy. (*He crosses to* FDR) You'd better get ready, Franklin.

FDR Jimmy—

JIMMY I've got them, Father.

(JIMMY *takes the braces from the desk and goes behind the screen with* FDR. HOWE *takes a step toward the screen and calls over*)

HOWE Franklin, I want to take another crack at you about the finish of the speech.

FDR (*Back of the screen*) Louie, not again.

HOWE Yes, again. Listen, Franklin, this phrase of Proskauer's is a rich one, and I think you're murdering it by not using it at the finish.

FDR (*Back of the screen*) It's close enough to the finish.

HOWE I think it ought to be the last thing you say. "I give you—the Happy Warrior of the Political Battlefield—Al Smith." Period. Crash.

FDR (*Back of the screen*) I don't think so. Period. Crash.

HOWE You're wrong. It's a sock phrase and will stick. It ought to be the punch line.

ELEANOR Franklin, may I say a word?

FDR (*Back of the screen*) Certainly. If you're going to agree with me.

ELEANOR Then I've nothing to say.

FDR (*Back of the screen, annoyed*) That's hardly a sign of wifely devotion.

HOWE Your being here and doing this is the most important thing. I only feel you're losing the value of the last minute or two of a good speech.

FDR (*Back of the screen*) Louie—I'm not sold on changing it. I'm sorry.

HOWE Further deponent sayeth not.

(*At that moment* FDR *appears with* JIMMY *from behind the screen*)

JIMMY Did I get it too tight, Father?

FDR I don't think so, Jimmy. No, that's fine.

(*At this moment* SARA ROOSEVELT *enters. The noise is suddenly louder.*)

SARA Franklin, they hardly let me through to you—

FDR Ma*ma,* ever the lady. You came in just at the right time —just as I stepped into my pants.

SARA Oh, Franklin—

FDR Welcome to the smoke-filled back room of politics.

SARA That howling mob outside is frightening.

FDR That howling mob consists of ladies and gentlemen conducting the business of democracy.

SARA How anything of consequence can be accomplished out of such a babble is a miracle.

FDR Ma*ma*—I'm all for noisy congregations. God help us if our conventions ever turn into high school pageants.

SARA Franklin, this is hardly the time to give me lessons in politics. I wanted only a moment to say God bless you.

FDR (*Simply*) He has given me many blessings.

(SARA *kisses him*)

SARA And, Franklin, speak out loudly and clearly.

(SARA *exits*)

HOWE Franklin, if I know Ma*ma,* in a couple of months she'll be working on a political primer. (*He looks at his watch*) I know this is awful—but I'm getting nervous.

ELEANOR And I have dropped three stitches.

FDR Sweet's taking a long time for a seconding speech—

HOWE He's only been on a few minutes. It just seems long.

(*The noise swells as the door burst open. The* POLICEMAN *is gripping* DALY)

DALY Mr. Howe—Mr. Howe—for God's sake, Miss LeHand, will you tell this man I belong here!

MISSY (*To* POLICEMAN) He does. He does.

(*The* POLICEMAN *unhands* DALY, *who moves into the room, excited*)

DALY Sorry I got panicky. Mr. Howe, you ought to get ready. The crowd is enormous and busting with excitement. Senator Walsh says it's time to get Mr. Roosevelt to the platform.

HOWE Missy—will you check the press handouts. Take Daly here with you for anything you need.

MISSY Right. (*Crosses to* FDR, *shakes his hand*) Boss, I know you'll be tremendous.

FDR Thanks, Missy. For everything.

(MISSY *starts for the door*)

DALY Good luck, Mr. Roosevelt—and to you, Mrs. Roosevelt—and to you, Elliott.

JIMMY James—Jimmy.

DALY Yes—thank you.

HOWE Okay, Daly. Good luck to you.

(DALY *waves and goes out with* MISSY)

FDR Jimmy, are you all set?

JIMMY Yes, Father. In my mind I have gone over it a hundred times. (*He smiles*) You make the speech, and I'll worry about everything else.

FDR (*With a laugh*) That's my son—man of iron. (*Now* FDR *leans over his legs*) Better check the braces. (*He clicks them into place—turns them with his hands and then releases them, leaving his knees limp again.* JIMMY *brings the crutches over*) They should be fine. Jimmy, if I slip, pick me up in a hurry.

(ELEANOR *comes to him and they caress each other*)

FDR (*He takes the crutches from Jimmy*) I'm ready. Jimmy—battle stations!

(JIMMY *starts to push the chair as* DALY *bursts in excitedly*)

DALY Mr. Roosevelt—

The Curtain Falls

SCENE THREE

Scene: The scene reveals the platform in Madison Square Garden. We are looking toward the rear platform. Facing us are huge drapes of bunting and pictures of Wilson and Jefferson. Stage front is the speaker's lectern, about twenty feet from the rear, where are grouped FDR *in his wheel chair,* JIMMY, *holding the crutches next to him, the other children,* ELEANOR ROOSEVELT, SARA ROOSEVELT, MISSY, LOUIE HOWE, *and the* POLICEMAN.

At rise: At the lectern is a SPEAKER. *Next to him is* SENATOR WALSH *of Montana, the Chairman. The crowd noise swells, loud and turbulent. It comes from all sides. There is no microphone, and the speakers must yell to be heard. It is bedlam as the* SPEAKER *tries to be heard.*

WALSH (*Banging gavel and screaming*) Ladies and Gentlemen! Please—give the speaker your attention—

(*There is some measure, small but noticeable, of attention*)

SPEAKER (*Also yelling*) There is a good deal of mail accumulating for the delegates in the Convention post office—and we urge you, please, to pick up your mail. It's getting very crowded. Please pick up your mail! Thank you!

(*There is cheering and screaming again.* WALSH *takes the gavel*)

WALSH (*After hammering the audience into some quiet*) We will continue with the calling of the roll. Connecticut!

VOICE (*From the pit*) Connecticut, the Nutmeg State, yields to the great Empire State of New York!

(*An enormous cheer and more yelling*)

WALSH (*Banging for quiet*) Ladies and Gentlemen! (*He hammers away with his gavel and finally gets some attention*) The Chair recognizes the Honorable Franklin D. Roosevelt of the State of New York!

(*As he says this, there is applause.* JIMMY *hands* FDR *the crutches; he gets to his feet and then, proud, smiling and confident, he starts to walk on his crutches to the lectern, as the applause mounts in intensity. Slowly, but strongly and surely,* FDR *walks those ten great steps. The cheering starts—whistles, screams, and rebel yells—and the band plays "Sidewalks of New York."* FDR *reaches the lectern and hands the crutches to* JIMMY, *who takes them and steps down. The screaming crowd continues to sound off.* FDR *stands there, holding the lectern with his left hand. Now he waves his right hand at the crowd in that familiar gesture. He smiles broadly, basking in the warmth of this genuine and whole-hearted tribute to his appearance, his courage and his future. The cheering continues as*

The Curtain Falls